To Rae!

Swimming UPstream

My Journey from Adversity to Hope, Inspiration
& a BIG LIFE *with* Winter the Dolphin

Live inspired!

Da Y

Psalm 32:8

DAVID P. YATES

Scripture quotations taken from The Holy Bible, New International Version® NIV®
Copyright © 1973 1978 1984 2011 by Biblica, Inc. TM
Used by permission. All rights reserved worldwide.

Paperback (B&W) ISBN 978-0-578-36811-5
Paperback (color) ISBN: 979-8-449-22271-8

Published by Dolphin Tell Productions, LLC
Palm Harbor, Florida, USA

Cover picture: Bob Talbot
Cover design: Ebook Launch

David P. Yates is the former CEO of the IRONMAN Group (IRONMAN Triathlon company) and Clearwater Marine Aquarium, home of the *Dolphin Tale* movies. Both CEO roles gave David a platform to reach millions with life-changing hope and inspiration, his life-calling. This book is for those wanting to shed themselves of fear and anxiety and lead the BIG LIFE God calls us to … helping others.

David is Co-Producer/Executive Producer of the #1 box office hit *Dolphin Tale* and its sequel, *Dolphin Tale 2*, the Warner Bros.-based Alcon Entertainment major motion pictures that star Morgan Freeman, Harry Connick Jr., Ashley Judd, Kris Kristofferson, Nathan Gamble, Cozi Zuehlsdorff and Austin Highsmith. David also directed and wrote the documentary *Winter, the Dolphin That Can* and the web series *Winter the Dolphin - Saving Winter*. David has won multiple Emmy Awards and other filmmaking and CEO awards. He and his beautiful wife Joan reside in Palm Harbor, Florida and have four grown children and two awesome grandchildren, all destined for great things.

David is available for public speaking, nonprofit consulting and personal coaching. Learn more at DavidYatesInspire.com or email him at David@DavidYatesInspire.com.

This book is dedicated to my amazing children,
Joshua, Christopher, Jordan, and Tiffany, our daughter-in-law, Andrea,
and our awesomely handsome grandsons Finley Jett and Murphy
Maverick.
Find your BIG LIVES.

And to my awesome wife, Joan, the love of my life, who led her own **BIG
LIFE**, putting up with my ups and downs as I found my **BIG LIFE**.

I met David when I was cast in *Dolphin Tale* at 12 years old. Now, ten years later, he's like my second dad. David doesn't sleep—every minute of every day is spent pouring into the lives of children and families inspired by the Clearwater Marine Aquarium, countless souls whose names and stories David knows by heart. David inspires me with his work ethic and sheer vision but does so in a way that makes me believe that same purpose lives inside of me. His ability to encourage me both deeply and disarmingly has set me straight countless times over the past decade. I only hope every single reader gets a chance to know David, but this book is without a doubt the next best thing.

—Cozi Zuehlsdorff, *Dolphin Tale* and Disney actor

I have known David extremely well for over a decade, yet reading this book, I learned things about him and his journey that I never knew before, and I'm even prouder to call him my friend and mentor. Reading *Swimming UPstream* had me sobbing more times than I could count, and that's saying something for a woman who made her career crying on cue! This book and David's willingness to share his heart, struggles, and overcoming triumphs made me feel like I can take on the world! I know this book will help so many people and inspire those already living Big Lives to reach for even bigger dreams. It certainly caused me to dream even bigger than I already was. David uses this quote in the book, but I've always said that if David Yates wakes up in the morning and sees a mountain in his path, he thinks, *No problem, I'll just move it*. And that "can-do" attitude is what has allowed David to reach so many of his dreams. I can't wait to see the impact this book has on the world. Because if it's anything like the impact David has had on my own life, the world is getting ready to become much more hopeful and inspired!

—Austin Highsmith, *Dolphin Tale* and film & TV actor

Thank you for giving me a life, David. Winter has reminded me that you should never let your disabilities stop you from accomplishing your dreams.

—Levi Larochelle – autism overcomer

David encourages me and makes me happy with Winter the dolphin messages. He gives me hope.

—Stephanie Evans – double organ transplant survivor

Listen, you keep on asking me to write a foreword in just one paragraph, but I can't in good conscience write it. Not because I don't have stuff to say; it's actually quite the opposite! I have SO MUCH to say, and to sum it up in one measly paragraph is a disservice to David and the readers! He's just an overall incredible individual that requires a whole book to sum up all of his career and character achievements. If only someone were to actually take the time and write a book detailing ALL of David's brilliance and accomplishments. Now, that would be a best seller for sure! I would buy that in a heartbeat! It could potentially be the best purchase an individual could make! (That good enough, Yates? Now, where's the check?)

—Nathan Gamble, *Dolphin Tale* and film & TV actor

ACKNOWLEDGMENTS

To the thousands of men, women and children I have met through IRON-MAN and Clearwater Marine Aquarium who have inspired me with their courage and determination. Without those experiences, my life would not be full.

Special thanks to:

Winter the dolphin. We did this together. Rest in peace, sweet girl ...

Allison Zuehlsdorff for amazing editing that makes me look like a real writer.

Ken Overman of BiographyMasters.com for editing, writing and design services. Also, to Eli Gonzalez for supplemental writing.

Joan Yates for proofing her husband's writing!

Sid and Rosalie Bullington, for raising nine great kids, including my wife.

Bob Miller, Jerry Starkweather, Dave Meylink, and Brad Bauman, who each in-spired a lost young man growing up in small-town Iowa.

Bill Stewart, who came into my life and altered its course just when I needed it.

The entire team at Alcon Entertainment for backing the Dolphin Tale dream.

My Dolphin Tale actors and dear friends Cozi Zuehlsdorff, Nathan Gamble, and Austin Highsmith, proving that "Family is Forever."

Lou Sloger, for counsel and advice on this book.

The amazing IRONMAN and Clearwater Marine Aquarium volunteers, who make the world a better place.

My brothers, my stepsister, my stepbrother, and my moms, Carolyn and Polly.

My father, Loren Yates, who set a humble example of looking out for the small guy or gal.

Craig Hatkoff, for being one of the first to see the power of Winter's story.

To the three ultimate BIG LIVES and what They did ... In the beginning, God created the heavens and the earth ... Genesis 1:1

INTRODUCTION

Swimming upstream ... it's really the story of my life, and also everyone you will read about in the following pages. I had to go against the current to achieve my life successes. But I found them. My two major career moves have been real Kilimanjaro experiences, during which I witnessed how hope made both children and adults overcomers after their lives imploded. I've worked with dying children lying in hospital beds, suicidal soldiers, abused children, Gold Star families and parents who brought us their children to complete their dying wish. Not just a few, but thousands and even tens of thousands. I am blessed to have had two careers that helped bring hope and inspiration to many. That's all I could have hoped for. However, it didn't just happen.

Getting there was a process that started with my decision to live a life of intentional purpose. I knew I wanted to live a BIG LIFE, and, for that, I would have to cast off the fear and anxiety that were the hallmarks of my childhood. In my heart, I felt I was destined for a BIG LIFE. Now all I had to do was put my head down and begin swimming upstream to where my hopes and dreams were. My BIG LIFE lay waiting.

Winter the dolphin playing with a young overcomer

9

All of us are on a journey with many surprising twists and turns. Consider your own life and ask yourself if it has gone the way you thought it would. If it hasn't, relax. That makes you normal, just like me. Who wants a sterile, overly planned life? Not me, and I hope you don't either. Look, even your GPS makes mistakes, doesn't it? Ever map out a trip only to find you're on some unknown road? Or that you steered to an unexpected tollbooth? Take heart; what disturbs your life now can be a motivator for change.

I began writing this book while I was CEO of the Clearwater Marine Aquarium (CMA), where most assumed I would finish my career. As of this writing, CMA is on a significant path, having become a global powerhouse in the world of marine life rescue, education and life-changing inspiration through the story of Winter the dolphin and the *Dolphin Tale* movies. As the guy who led the way with a new $80 million facility, having expanded our work around the world with two films and a likely TV show in the works, one would think I would be at CMA for life. After all, I should coast to the end of my career while gliding into retirement, right? Nope. Instead, I took a bold—and most would say, stunning—step and submitted my resignation. Why? Because I have a few more dreams to chase. The public, my friends, and the media could not believe it. They thought I was joking. Some, even those close to me, thought I was nuts. Well, that may be true, but I have other mountains to climb. And I bet you do as well. With the onslaught of COVID, we have all been shaken one way or another. We've all had to climb out of the valley this virus has led us through. Let's move beyond it and push our lives forward.

Through the narrative of my life story, you will see how you can turn your detours and valleys into real opportunities by:

- Breaking free from your past to change the trajectory of your life. Warning: You may have to swim upstream. Get ready.
- Turning off the pause button of your life and switching it to fast-forward.
- Saying "no" to the status quo of fear and anxiety and saying "yes" to doing something big and bold.
- Saying goodbye to the naysayers in your life.
- Having a purpose, one bigger than you think.
- Living ... a BIG LIFE!

Here's the deal. God uses ordinary people to do extraordinary things. It's that simple, and my story will illustrate that fact. I started as an accountant and ended up living the dream you'll read about in the following pages. And by the way, what I call living a "BIG LIFE" doesn't mean trying to measure up to someone else's BIG LIFE. You won't do the things I did in my life, and vice versa. What it does mean is:

Living a life without artificial limitations placed on you by yourself or someone else, and reimagining the magnitude of the impact your life can make on *others*.

I'm convinced that everyone wants to live a more impactful life. Well, the good news is that regardless of how your life has rolled out so far, you can change your trajectory at any time. Don't wait. Put your head down and start swimming! I've learned to take my experiences—both good and bad—and use what they have taught me to move my life forward. Throughout this book, I'll be sharing the lessons I've learned so that you can also move on to a more purpose-filled life.

You'll find that many of my "words of wisdom" are found in the Bible because I'm not smart enough to figure out life by myself. I'm a believer in Jesus Christ, and that is who I follow. To me, the principles I share have everything to do with knowing Him. I don't preach. I simply say what is real to me. No matter who you are, these principles will apply. I came from a troubled background, but through hard work, a renewed attitude and rejecting the destructive path of victimhood, I got past it. Most importantly, I had the help of others. Then, with that help, I went on to build multiple global inspirational brands, took on the Olympic Federation system, faced off with a state government system, fended off an attack from Scientology, produced network TV shows and two major motion pictures. And I started as an accountant. Yep, a boring "I-know-my-numbers" accountant! (*Note: Not saying accountants are boring. No letters, please.*)

For whatever reason, I have been put on the global stage more than once, and the journey that led to those great experiences sprung from both inspiring and difficult periods in my past. Simply put, if a disabled dolphin and a triathlon race can completely change my life and the lives of millions of others, the catalyst for change in your own life could be just around the corner.

As you read my story, you'll find that no matter who you are or where you've been, you can still alter your course. Like zeroing in on a moon landing, a one-degree change of your trajectory will land you in the place you want to be.

As of this writing, I have spent a total of 24 years with two great organizations, the IRONMAN Triathlon Company (now known as the IRONMAN Group) and the Clearwater Marine Aquarium. For twenty of those years, I was the CEO of those organizations. Every brand I built, or helped to create, carries the same message: *hope* and *purpose*. I wasn't afraid to swim upstream when I had to. That's my thing. It's also what this book is about.

Kick fear aside and let's get going. Find your BIG LIFE.

With Winter and Hope, Clearwater Marine Aquarium, 2020

TABLE OF CONTENTS

1

A LETTER AND A PHONE CALL – FROM THE FUTURE

A Letter

Dear David,

I just want to say that you are by far one of the most gracious people I have the blessing to have in my life. You have been there for my family and me since I received my arm from Winter at Clearwater Marine Aquarium almost five years ago. What an amazing, life-altering experience that was! Thank you!

The impact you have made in my life is unexplainable, and I can't thank you enough for everything you have done for not only me but for all of the other children you have brought to the aquarium. Your courage to keep Winter, no matter how many times others tried to discourage you, gives me great comfort. Knowing there is a person out there who would do anything for others with a difference gives me courage.

David Yates, you are my Superhero!

Love,
Anni Emmert, prosthetic arm user

No, I'm not a superhero … Anni's story will come later in the book. But first, I'll tell you a bit about me and how my life led to that letter.

A Phone Call

June 2010 – Clearwater, Florida: *"David, we have a greenlight!"*

With those six words, two major motion pictures, *Dolphin Tale* and *Dolphin Tale 2*, were launched on the path to reality. That news from a good friend at Alcon Entertainment would change the course of history for Clearwater Marine Aquarium and my life. It would also launch a multibillion-dollar economic impact throughout the Clearwater, Florida, area, create thousands of jobs and begin the healing process for tens of thousands of sick and disabled kids worldwide, maybe millions. All it took were those six words.

After I hung up the phone, I considered the long road that led to that moment. We had spent nearly three years of grinding pre-development work on the movie, and despite numerous setbacks, we were victorious against all odds. Best of all, we would film *Dolphin Tale* at our facility! Wow. Who gets to do that?

As the CEO of the Clearwater Marine Aquarium (CMA) and a producer of the movies, I had a pretty good idea of what was to come as we took Winter the dolphin's incredible story to the world via the big screen. I'd already seen Winter change many lives, one at a time (you'll read Winter's story later on). What was impossible for many to see was how sizable the impact would be. Millions reached with life-changing inspiration, and hundreds of thousands pulled out of despair. This would be a *movement*, not only a movie.

I walked to my office window, gazed over the small, struggling aquarium, and thought, *Bad news is about to meet its greatest enemy, Hope!* It would come in the unlikely form of a rescued dolphin named Winter and travel throughout the world as a powerful symbol of overcoming life's struggles.

Few believed I could pull off landing a movie, but I refused to listen to the naysayers. Both inside and outside our organization, more than a few people told me I was wasting my own time as well as Clearwater Marine Aquarium's time by chasing a Hollywood "pipe dream." In some ways, it was me against the world. I believed in the power of Winter's story and the fantastic marine life rescue work being done at CMA, and I had a dream. A big dream. Now that we were about to produce a movie, we were also about to bring an inspirational movement to the global scene. *Watch out, Oprah!* CMA's limited physical size momentarily camouflaged the worldwide impact Winter's story would have as it grabbed the hearts of hundreds of millions over the next decade in nearly every country of the world.

Winter the Dolphin

Our humble little education and marine life rescue center was about to be invaded by the big wide world, and it was my job to prepare us. To make it happen, I would have to draw upon everything I knew and then some. We would play host to a few little-known A-listers. Maybe you've heard of them? Morgan Freeman, Harry Connick, Jr., Ashley Judd and Kris Kristofferson. Pretty cool, to say the least. I'd always strived for a significant purpose for my life. Little did I know, it was about to get bigger, much bigger, far upstream from where I started.

A snapshot of my life as a teenager would have predicted a life of failure, not of success. I've learned a lot from my past. So, at this point, I'll take you on a brief journey back to where it all began. I'll show you that if I can make it through some disastrous times and wind up living a BIG LIFE, so can you.

2

HARDSHIPS: MY ROCKY CHILDHOOD

Okay, so maybe Anni was partially right, as I did want to be a superhero. Yes, that's a stupid picture of me as a five-year-old. Though I can assure you I'm an average guy, I really did want to be Superman when I was a kid. What red-blooded American boy didn't? So, with that suit on, I proudly climbed out onto the ledge of a second-story window in our home. I was all ready to jump. I knew I could fly. *I just knew it.* Fortunately, some adults knew differently and stopped me before I killed myself.

I never stopped dreaming, though, because someday I knew I would fly. I was right, but it took a while because, behind that veneer of innocent belief, there was a lot of turbulence wreaking havoc inside of me. It would be decades until I earned my wings.

"All these years, the people said 'He's actin' like a kid.'
He did not know he could not fly, and so he did."
~ Guy Clark – The Cape

A Rough Start

Schiz·o·phre·ni·a – A long-term mental disorder of a type involving a break-down in the relation between thought, emotion, and behavior, leading to with-drawal from reality and personal relationships into fantasy and delusion, and a sense of mental fragmentation.

My biological mother—Carolyn Yates—had schizophrenia. Severe schizo-phrenia. She was unable to properly care for my brothers and me, even though she tried. Her schizophrenia began manifesting itself during her early twenties while she was having and raising us kids, and it escalated into a lifetime of severe mental illness. Her illness would define the rest of her life and, to one extent or another, the lives of my brothers and me. I was later told her condition had worsened around the time I was born. It was hard on everyone, particular-ly Dad, who was a busy small-town M.D.

Loren & Carolyn Yates' engagement picture – 1953

Look closely at this picture of Carolyn. You would never suspect a lifetime of schizophrenia. She is beautiful and looks normal, but mental illness is a hidden epidemic. Despite recent gains in public awareness, few understand the seriousness of this problem and how it devastates families. For most of my adult life, I had no idea how to relate to Carolyn and her issues. She suffered, and I felt helpless as to what to do. I do not blame her for any problems it created for me. Schizophrenia wasn't her fault. I only wish I had the chance to know my mother as she was before she got sick.

Carolyn was unintentionally abusive, but not in the physical sense. Instead, her abuse manifested as a lack of supervision. It wasn't her fault. Allow a mentally ill parent to give a three-year-old the whole world, and you get what I'm talking about. Without consistent parenting, I perfected the art of getting into trouble without even trying. You might say I was destined to reign as the Yates MVP in this skill set. Without intervention, I was guaranteed a life of tragedy. As a toddler, I would occasionally walk right out of the house and go wherever I wanted. Sometimes I wound up at the grocery store on the corner until someone eventually took me back home.

As Carolyn's illness and irrationality grew worse, her marriage headed south. Dad tried to make it work, but Carolyn's condition was simply too difficult to live with. Not surprisingly, when I was around five, they ended up in divorce. In those days, the "nurturing" mother almost always gained custody of the kids in a divorce. Since Carolyn was the mom, she kept all of us in a small town called Grove, Oklahoma. Dad remarried and moved to another small town in Iowa. I know Dad felt terrible about leaving us, but with the courts the way they were, he must have felt there was no chance of gaining custody.

On the Lam

After moving to Iowa, Dad sent money to Oklahoma to Carolyn for rent. One day, he received a call from her landlord saying the rent was past due. Driven by her severe mental illness and conflict avoidance, Carolyn made a run for it. She piled all of us in the car, and, just like that, we were on the lam with no idea where we were going. We were just kids experiencing the unraveling of a seriously ill person. A few days later, we landed somewhere in Dallas, Texas.

Finally, Dad located the four of us, and on his second visit, grabbed us and hightailed it to Iowa. I don't remember much about the trip, but looking back, it sure seemed like kidnapping. If the Amber Alert was around then, I guess we would have been on it. You don't just grab four kids without having legal custody and take off to another state without a bunch of attorneys getting involved. Anyway, it was the right thing to do because Dad knew we were at risk.

There were court proceedings, of course. Carolyn's sister, Aunt Mary Jo, tes-tified against her. She knew that Carolyn was unable to take care of us. Every-one knew it. A portion of the court decree read as follows:

> *"The Court finds that there has been sufficient change in the mental condition of the Plaintiff, sufficient to find that she is not competent, capable, or fit to take care, custody, and control of the four minor children of the parties."*

With those words, it was a new day for the Yates kids, yet a dagger was driv-en deep into Carolyn's heart, a wound from which she never recovered. Mary Jo is a hero to me and my brothers for doing what she did. That was in the mid-1960s. In those days, few fathers secured full custody of their children, but Dad did. Carolyn's anger only deepened after that, and her mental condition spiraled further downward. Soon after the judgment, Carolyn retreated to the town she lived in most of her life: Muskogee, Oklahoma.

Carolyn struggled to hold a normal conversation and had to live with as-sistance during the last 60 years of her life. It was difficult to watch her schizo-phrenia manifest itself in a constant battle going on in her head. She believed that all of her boys would one day rule heaven and told us we would all become "gods." She also heard voices and had loud conversations with them, causing problems in many of the facilities in which she lived. She tried going to church but got so nervous she stopped attending. My half-brother Mike took up the task of caring for her over the years, as he lived nearby, and he did a great job. We are all grateful to him.

I learned two things about mental illness from Carolyn: it is devastating, and it needs a much brighter light shone on it. Carolyn deserved a better life than she got. She died two years before this book's publication. As I write this, I am working on a movie about schizophrenia that I hope to honor her with.

Yates Boys & Carolyn – Circa 1970

Emotional Damage

When I was four, I decided to get attention by ingesting a bottle of chewable aspirin. Somehow, I got to the hospital, where my dad pumped my stomach and saved my young life. Up to this point, my life was (predictably) a pure disaster. There's no other way to put it. Anyone would have said that as a young kid, I was heading for trouble—then it got worse.

Dad met his second wife, Polly, in Oklahoma, and they married before moving to a small town in Northwest Iowa. Okay, that's redundant because all towns in Iowa are small. We first lived in Hawarden, then a year later, we moved to Rock Valley. Both towns are nestled in the northwest corner of the state. I didn't like either of them at first, but then again, I'm not sure I could have liked anything at that age. Later, though, I grew to love our new life, especially in Rock Valley. Like its name, Rock Valley became my rock, and I needed one. I also acquired an extended family.

The Yates boys merged with a stepsister (Katie), a stepbrother (Elton) and a stepmother (Polly). We became one big, blended family overnight. Our half-brother, Mike, lived with Carolyn, not with us. Having been lumped together so fast, we had a few challenges, but overall, we got along and still do.

The big issue for me was my relationship with Polly, which quickly became caustic. That was not surprising. She had inherited an out-of-control five-year-old boy and didn't know how to handle him. She was a uniquely rigid person with little imagination and ran things by the book. Let's just say that early in our relationship, little David Yates and Polly did not hit it off.

When it came to creative thinking, Polly struggled. When one of her sisters told her she wanted to be a fiction writer, Polly commented, "Why would you write something that is not true?" While that may be funny, you get my point. When you take an adult with that frame of mind, hand her four new kids to go with the two she already had, you're asking for trouble. The *Hindenburg* was waiting for a spark to ignite. And ignite, it did.

Things quickly went south between Polly and me, and she consulted a psychiatrist for advice about what to do with me. Among other things, he told her to be extremely firm with me. I've always wanted to find that guy so I could beat him! Considering her natural rigidity, Polly had no problem being firm. She was instinctively firm to start with and didn't need encouragement from anyone else. After getting advice from the psychiatrist, she became more rigid in her dealings with me, thinking that was the right thing to do. That's how it was for most of my childhood. Too many emotional and physical altercations.

Year after year, I craved love that Polly couldn't provide. She, in turn, demanded respect I refused to give. It was an endless cycle that led to juvenile delinquency and the dodging of consequences. I would lie, cheat and steal and get away with it. By age 12, a few select friends and I were in the habit of breaking into local stores, and because I believed no one cared for me, I had every intention of doing more of the same. What else was there to live for? I was an emotional outcast, but I was also a pro at hiding it.

Then Dad stepped in. Because he was an M.D., medications flowed somewhat freely at our house (legally, of course), and one day he prescribed a powerful drug called Haldol to calm me down. Much to his chagrin, I don't remember it making me feel any calmer, but I do remember having consistent stomach pain. Later in life, when I told a pharmacist friend that I had been given Haldol, her jaw dropped. That's how I found out it was a primary antipsychotic drug. If that was Dad's way of controlling me, I'm sure he did it because he was concerned. Seeing my behavior, he probably assumed I was becoming psychotic, like Carolyn.

As for me, I grew up fearing I would develop Carolyn's mental illness. It seemed inevitable. My emotional struggles and profound nervousness at a young age only compounded those fears. I remember Dad once telling me that schizophrenia wasn't passed on genetically. Still, I didn't believe him. We now know children can inherit an increased predisposition to schizophrenia from a parent. Thankfully that didn't happen to me, but at that time, my fears were real, and I was afraid there was nothing I would be able to do to quiet them.

With my young life already on the rocks, no rational person would bet I would end up living any semblance of a BIG LIFE. Vegas wouldn't have taken the odds, that's for sure! I know it's likely that many reading this book are living in a disaster right now. If you are, and if you think your life is over, *it's not!* God can provide a different plan for your life. Read on.

Spiraling Downward

As time passed, I grew more and more angry and depressed, and I didn't know how to deal with it; too many confrontations and too much anger with no outlet. I was overwhelmed. By the time I entered Rock Valley Junior High, I was in full rebellion. I quickly established myself as a rabble-rouser. I was constantly in trouble, always finding my way to the nearest underage keg party. I was a rebellious little jerk.

At this point, I could barely sit down long enough to eat a meal and was still on Haldol. I was a nervous wreck and getting worse every day. But what could I do? Even though I was a victim of my circumstances, what use would it be to play the victim card? It would get me nowhere. In the end, it would be me who suffered the consequences. I thank God I had the sense to realize I had to pick myself up and move on. After all, I wasn't the first kid to have a troubled childhood, and I wouldn't be the last.

Ultimately, when all has been said and done, I hold nothing against Polly. She went from two kids to six overnight, and who could deal with getting a hold of me at age five? Later, she became a godly lady who worked hard and meant well, but it just never worked out between her and me. That happens. I'll leave it at that.

We've all been hurt, disappointed, angered or let down. For some, the hurt was legitimate with significant, debilitating effects. The question is, what are we going to do about it? Stay angry? Look for revenge? Or will we see the situation for what it is and alter the dangerous trajectory of our lives? Do what I did. Choose instead to live a full, purpose-filled life. Break the shackles of your past! Are you stuck? Get unstuck.

Proverbs 17:9 says, *"Whoever would foster love covers over an offense."* That also applies to you. If you trade contempt for loving others and yourself, you will find yourself on the road to success.

A Bend in the Road

Dad had a heart attack at the young age of 44. As a small-town doctor on call 24/7, he was continuously overworked, and like many in his day, he was also a heavy smoker. Many doctors smoked in the '60s and '70s. Blame it on the Marlboro Man, I guess, though ironically, the actor who played the role was a non-smoker.

After my dad recovered, his doctor told him to consider leaving the small-town doctor life and find a less stressful medical position. He agreed, and in 1974 he packed up our family and moved to Lubbock, a good-sized town in hot, dry, and flat West Texas. It suited him perfectly. When we lived in Iowa, he had often threatened to fasten a snow shovel to the front of his car and drive straight south until someone asked him what the shovel was for. "That," he said, "is where we'd make our new home." Ha!

Thankfully, he never had to do that. He finally found a warm locale with a pace of work that matched the weather. He minimized his smoking and kept regular hours in his position at the new Texas Tech University Medical School.

I, however, was furious.

Fourteen is difficult enough for any American boy but ripping me away from the only life I knew, a life my identity was based on, was unforgivable to me at that time. Those were the days before social media, so except for an occasional letter and a rare phone call, I lost communication with most of my Iowa friends. I was beyond angry. Emotionally, I feared I was becoming Carolyn.

Lubbock was the opposite of everything I knew. I went from a small town of less than 2,000 to a city of 200,000, from a class of less than 50 to a class of around 600. Put into perspective, my new high school was larger than the entire town of Rock Valley. Talk about culture shock. Instead of being a known entity on a small junior high school campus, I was one guy in a very big place and out of my element. Yet, I soon discovered Lubbock was more than warm weather, cotton crops and dust. It was great for its southern hospitality and hometown heroes like Buddy Holly and Mac Davis. As difficult as it felt, I was learning to move on with life at a young age, even if I didn't like the change it brought. That fall, I went to Evans Jr. High School for 9th grade. To help me find my bearings, I dove right into athletics. Although I still missed Iowa, half-way through the school year, I started to feel a little at home. That said, "Just when you start to feel comfortable ..."

Despite the slower pace and better climate, Dad required a quadruple heart bypass. Open-heart surgery is always a big deal, but 1974 was practically the dark age of that technology. Dad assumed he wouldn't survive the operation, so he wrote a letter saying goodbye to us. I still have it, but I never believed he would die. After all, Dad was Dad and would always be around, right? That time I was right. He pulled through just fine.

Around that time, Polly and Dad found their faith in Christ, which was intense and compelling to them. Every time the doors of Melanie Park Baptist Church on Indiana Avenue opened, we were there. But I was still angry, and because of all my unresolved issues, my rebellion only grew. I had already been arrested for violating Lubbock's teenage curfew with some friends. We were at a party and had decided to roam the area at around 3:00 a.m. when we were spotted by the police. Being the intelligent, well-mannered kids that we were, we did what any American kids would do. *We ran.* The police chased us, and as a couple of us were climbing a fence, we were nabbed to the voice of "Nice try, Spider-Man." I would have preferred he called us Superman, but later in life, I worked with Marvel comics, so maybe there was a little foreshadowing going on. In any case, since I was a proverbial train wreck waiting to happen, it's not surprising that it did. It was a car wreck, to be exact.

As a rather stupid ninth grader without a driver's license, I snuck my brother's car out with a friend and crashed it into a car at the local mall. They took the driver to the hospital, and guess who was the on-duty doctor in this particular hospital emergency room and at this particular time? Yep, my dad. Talk about being busted. Dad had to decline to see the patient since I was the cause of the wreck. As stupid as it was, this event was a turning point in my life. I considered that accident a wake-up call from God. I was grounded for what seemed multiple lifetimes (I think I grew a beard during this stretch of punishment), but it gave me plenty of time to think about where my life was headed. My childhood pranks were turning into adult crimes. I needed intervention, and I had gotten one—from God.

I went from a life of partying and troublemaking to attending a youth group. My friends didn't know what had come over me, but when I started to hang out with the churchgoer crowd, well, that changed a few relationships. Although my life was now getting on track in some positive ways, I was still only fourteen, and I had relied on popularity and hanging with the "in-crowd" as my anchor. When I walked away from that form of codependency, the bottom completely dropped out. I went through a couple of years of DEEP depression and didn't have a clue about how to deal with it. I had no parental relationships and no idea how to talk about my feelings.

That's when Bill Stewart entered my life. As it turns out, he was just in time. I needed a mentor in my life to keep me from falling back into self-destruction. Bill was our church youth group leader. He and his wife, Sarah, were raising seven children while living on his dinky youth pastor's salary. Still, they could not have been happier. They had found the key to life, and their lack of funds, while driving a run-down VW bus, didn't bother them a bit. Bill took an interest in me and some other guys who would become lifetime friends. They included Rodney Dunn, David Dale, David Ortiz and Gary Solesbee, among others. It was Bill's intervention in my life that changed its downward trajectory. He pulled me up when I was drowning, taught me how to begin swimming upstream to a new destination and stuck with me along the way. As for Bill, he has become a ridiculously successful businessman. He deserves it, as he has led his own BIG LIFE.

Surround yourself with positive, constructive people and lean into them. As my friend and pastor Kurt Parker says, "Show me your friends, and I'll show you your future." That is so true. Who you spend your time with will significantly influence what you achieve in life. We all know it. Hang around naysayers, and you'll go nowhere. I'm not telling you to throw away relationships with friends and family; I'm just saying to use discernment. Are the people you spend most of your time with helping you fly higher, or are they causing turbulence in your life? That's the $64,000 question (not including inflation).

Be like Bill. Make yourself available as a mentor and help change a life. Do it now, and expand your purpose.

Losing Dad

Four years after moving to Lubbock, the Yates family moved again. This time we went from Texas heat to Nebraska cold. Yikes! Dad accepted a position at Creighton University Medical School in Omaha, Nebraska. Suddenly, we were back up in the cold tundra of the north again. While the change was good for Dad's career, once again, my life took some unexpected twists and turns.

Mom, Dad, and my younger brother, Dan, moved in 1978. I followed the next summer. I had just graduated from Monterey High School in Lubbock. Around that time, I was offered track and field scholarships from some colleges. I accepted one at South Plains College just outside Lubbock and enrolled. During my first semester, I won the fall college meet, but I wasn't happy with the coach and decided to leave. Fortunately, I was offered a second scholarship—this one from Howard Payne University in Brownwood, Texas—but I changed my mind and never showed up. The truth is, I was still wandering, unsure of my roots. Instead, I went to Omaha for the summer of 1979 to stay with the family, and, as it often happens, I ended up staying longer than I planned. Much longer.

I had given up the other scholarships but had run in a few local races. Apparently, I was being observed because the head track coach at the University of Nebraska Omaha (UNO), asked if I would consider running for them. I said I would, but once again, life got in the way. This time it hit hard.

It was July 2, 1982. I'll never forget those twenty-four hours. It started when I got home from my college classes and my aunt Joyce told me Dad had another heart attack. Aunt Joyce had been staying with us for the summer. Polly was with Dad at Methodist Hospital. We were told we could see him the next day. I was concerned, of course, but because he had already survived one heart attack and had bypasses, I went to bed believing he would be fine and that I'd see him the next day.

Then came the call that shook me for years.

Although Dad had a minor heart attack earlier in the day, he suffered a massive one later that night. We got to the hospital in time to be with him for the last few hours of his life. At the young age of 53, Dad passed away, and a piece of my heart died also. As I write this, I am nearly ten years older than Dad was when he died. His death created an urgency within me to finish my life strong for however many days I have left. I often dream of the day we meet in heaven—when I can tell him what I did with my life and give him the credit he deserves. That day will come.

My father's death helped me focus on living a life of meaning and purpose. Now that you've heard about the impact my dad's death had on my life, think

27

about yourself. Regardless of your age, marital status, or circumstances, for what and for whom are you living? Don't wait for a tragedy to befall you to find out. Chart the course to your BIG LIFE now.

Looking Ahead

Since the NBA had not yet called me (I have no idea why), I decided to put my collegiate athletic endeavors aside and work my way through college at the University of Nebraska Omaha a great university with one of the top business schools in the country. I still had no idea what I would do, but I needed to get myself a career and stop majoring in recreational basketball and class skipping.

Meanwhile, I kept trying to dislodge the memory of my childhood traumas. I was still an emotional mess and very insecure. There was nothing to indicate that David Yates would have future success at Clearwater Marine Aquarium or anywhere else for that matter, yet I was determined to do first things first, and that meant getting through college and becoming an accountant. Wait—what? An accountant? Yes, I literally chose accounting because it was the first major listed alphabetically at our freshman orientation. How's that for a strategically planned life? Thank goodness "brain surgeon" wasn't first on the list. I would have single-handedly destroyed that profession.

I had no clue where I was going, and I had no vision for a successful future when I graduated. But starting with a degree in accounting seemed like a safe step in the right direction. Another critical step was to learn from the professionals around me and then add hard work to the education they were giving me.

"Winners embrace hard work.
They love the discipline of it, the trade-off they're making to win.
Losers, on the other hand, see it as punishment. And that's the difference."

~ Lou Holtz

3

UPS & DOWNS: MY EARLY CAREER EXPERIENCES

Life Lessons from Mrs. B - $500 to $55 million

"Formal education will make you a living;
self-education will make you a fortune."

~ Jim Rohn

I LOVE that quote because it is SO true. In college, we learn from books and studying, but real-life learning comes from our real-life experiences. When someone asks me about a particular person or event that changed my career trajectory, I immediately point to one fabulous person, Rose Blumkin, who hired me to work at her massive furniture store during my college years. Otherwise known as "Mrs. B," she was well under five feet tall and diminutive in stature. That, however, was the only small thing about her.

Mrs. B. immigrated to the United States in her twenties flat broke. She told me she never attended a day of school in her life and only learned English by asking her kids what they learned at school each day. Using a $500 loan from her brother in 1937 she began a classic rags-to-riches life story, founding what is now the world-renowned Nebraska Furniture Mart, a furniture store chain. In the early days, she sold furniture at such low prices that it outraged her competitors. Some sued her for violating Fair Trade Laws. Well, she won—and then sold the judge $1,400 worth of carpet! Ha. Her competitors then retaliated by calling for a boycott of her store and even convinced her vendors to stop supplying her. Not to be outsmarted, she went around them and bought outside the area. Eventually, this indomitable woman built the world's largest furniture store under one roof. Today there are multiple Nebraska Furniture Mart locations, and that original $500 investment now generates hundreds of millions of dollars each year. Wow!

She was so successful and trustworthy that Warren Buffett (yes, that Warren Buffett) bought her out in 1983 for $55 million, and without an audit! They sealed the deal on a handshake—known as the "Historic Omaha Handshake." I was there when Warren—I love coming off like we are on a first-name basis—stopped by to talk about the sale.

Mrs. B. worked until the age of 103, rarely missing a day, and died at 104. She was unstoppable. I had the blessing of watching her do her thing seven days a week, selling, selling, and selling—an authentic and inspiring rags-to-riches story. Mrs. B. was the ultimate master sales motivator, and she knew it. She also leveraged volume discounts and often told customers, "The more you buy, the more you save." And dang it if millions of customers didn't agree. That was a woman who, against all odds, rose to the top of the business community and became a nationally recognized success. Mrs. B. had no head start, no wealthy relative to fund her, and no formal education. Talk about swimming upstream! She was straightforward, and her story taught me all I needed to know about success.

Hard work plus a plan and an against-all-odds mentality will win every time. Mic drop.

Often success is just around the corner, but many of us give up before we get there. It's those who reject the give-up mentality that find success. I learned more by observing Mrs. B. than from anyone else in my life up to that point. Mrs. B.'s robust and persistent example showed me all I needed to succeed. I quietly watched the against-all-odds miracle woman, and thanks to her, my disoriented life gained a layer of success. She was a true disruptor, and it rubbed off on me. At the time, I had no idea how powerful the life lessons I learned from her would be, but very soon, they would start to play out.

Sweat it out. Hard work works. Half-baked work doesn't. We all know this, but how often do we slack off, knowing it won't turn out the way we want?

"How long will you lie there, you sluggard? When will you get up from your sleep? A little sleep, a little slumber, a little folding of the hands to rest—and poverty will come on you like a thief and scarcity like an armed man."
~ Proverbs 6:9-12

Ouch. Sometimes the Bible has stern words for us. Let's get to work.

I'm Going to Marry Who?

A few months before he died, Dad was the lead in a church musical at Westside Baptist Church in Omaha. Well-known author Calvin Miller pastored the church. It was 1982, and an awesome-looking woman named Joan was also singing in the musical. At one particular Sunday service, the pastor told the congregation to meet and greet others in the audience. Since she knew my dad, Joan walked over to say hello. I happened to be with my gregarious aunt Joyce, who was staying with us for the summer. When Joan shook my hand, Aunt Joyce turned to me and said, "David, you're going to marry that girl!"

I wish, I thought. But she really did say that.

My aunt was known to be quite the jester, but at that time, it didn't sound like she was joking. I blew off the comment, but two years later, on June 8, 1984, Aunt Joyce proved to be correct. I married Joan. Calvin Miller and his son-in-law, Lou Sloger, performed the ceremony. Lou and his wife, Melanie—Calvin's daughter—are close friends of ours to this day. Incidentally, my proposal to Joan was one of the wimpiest in history. It was so bad that Joan wasn't sure I proposed at all. What an idiot I was. I married a beautiful lady, and life seemed good. But as we have all experienced, when life seems to be on track, well, watch out! What happened next completely derailed me.

Shattered Dreams

"You're fired!" No, I'm not quoting Donald Trump. Wait, maybe I am. Let me explain. After I graduated from the University of Nebraska Omaha with a business and accounting degree, I went to work for one of the "BIG 8" accounting firms—Arthur Young & Company (today's Ernst & Young). We jokingly called ourselves "the other Arthur" since Arthur Andersen was the dominant international CPA firm of the day. Arthur Andersen was to CPAs what the New York Yankees were to kids growing up playing baseball. Top-of-the-mountain stuff.

I rose fast at Arthur Young and loved it. The Omaha office where I worked was small, with around 40 members on the tax and audit teams. I was on the audit side, and since most of our clients' businesses were relatively small, our Omaha staff was allowed to have greater responsibility than our larger offices with big clients. In just over a year, I was in charge of overseeing my first audit. It was a great way to start because I could dig into all aspects of a business and see the big picture.

All seemed good. Our first child, Joshua, was growing like a weed, and my career was rocking right along. Then life's dark side reared its ugly head. After nearly two years at Arthur Young and with a robust annual review and a raise a few months earlier, a number of us who were at the same level of experience were suddenly laid off. Entirely out of the blue.

Dev·as·ta·tion: to reduce to chaos, disorder, or helplessness.

Wow. What happened? I had done a great job, and I knew they liked me and my work. Apparently, they had been hemorrhaging clients and had to downsize at the level I was at. Wrong place, wrong time. What do I do now? I had to go home and tell Joan I was out of a job. We relied on my income, and the Arthur Young job was a dream come true. I was horrified about losing my job, and we had just had our first child. We had little savings, and my career had become my identity. *What now?*

Well, a little like Michael Keaton in the 1983 hit comedy of the same name, I became Mr. Mom while Joan took a part-time job. My out-of-work status was short, as I landed a position with a major construction conglomerate in Omaha called Peter Kiewit & Sons, Inc. It was a huge company and a significant next step in my career. The company had subsidiaries worldwide, and I was on the internal audit team based in the Kiewit Building. It was a lot of travel, but I enjoyed it.

I audited major construction projects in LA, Wyoming and Connecticut to ensure they were being conducted properly. Providentially, the knowledge I gained there would be indispensable in the next phase of my life, even though I didn't know it then.

Well, guess who else worked in the same building? None other than the Oracle of Omaha—the Bishop of Berkshire Hathaway—Mr. Warren Buffett. Yep, there he was again. Occasionally, Mr. Buffett would ride the elevator with us, and when he did, we would all shut up. We were hoping to hear the latest Buffett wisdom. Was he buying? Selling? I never picked up any of his global stock tips, but I did keep my eyes open for other career opportunities. I didn't feel I would be at Peter Kiewit & Sons, Inc. forever. Don't get me wrong, it was a great company, but I had landed there somewhat out of necessity, and I had this nagging feeling it was temporary. Turns out, my gut feeling was about to be right. After only nine months on the job, I got a job offer to work in Florida through a connection of one of my brothers. So in June 1987, off we went to the Sunshine State, leaving the Nebraska cold and our snow tires behind.

Perhaps many of you reading this have given up on leading a BIG LIFE and instead have become complacent. To you, I say, look at Michael Phelps, Christopher Reeve, Kodi Lee and the many other examples of courage and determination in overcoming life challenges. Let me encourage you. If you're alive (and you are), you still have time to strive for a BIG purpose.

From that point forward, what happened to me demonstrates how life's random detours can become some of the biggest opportunities. Use your own past to steer through the challenging times and turn them into successes.

"Sometimes, when you're in a dark place, you think you've been buried, but you've actually been planted."

~ Christine Caine

4

A NEW DREAM: THE IRONMAN YEARS

"He who takes no chances wins nothing."
~ Danish Proverb

New Beginnings

December 1989 – Tarpon Springs, Florida

*F*ive words. *"Congratulations, Blitz ... we did it!"* With that, a group of us from the consortium I now worked for in Florida were the new owners of the IRONMAN Triathlon, now known as the IRONMAN Group. The consortium was owned by an amazing family based just outside Tampa. Byron (Blitz) Fox and I had spent countless hours on the phone negotiating and many more conducting due diligence for the purchase. Now we were finally done, but it had taken months out of our lives, and we were both exhausted and ecstatic.

IRONMAN World Championship swim start

I couldn't have known it at the time, but I would spend the next ten or so years of my life developing the inspiring world of IRONMAN's global events and brands. I would be privileged to work side by side with thousands of amazing athletes. Some of them were chasing their athletic dreams while others were celebrating victory in overcoming a life challenge. Still others competed in memory of a loved one. They would vie for the chance to cross the hallowed finish line of the IRONMAN World Championship in Kona, Hawaii.

Julie Moss crawling to the finish line

Who can forget the legendary image of Julie Moss crawling to the finish line at the 1982 IRONMAN race? It was one of the greatest sports moments when raw courage and a refusal to give up put the new endurance race on the world map.

A Little Background

The idea for the first IRONMAN event, held in Hawaii in 1978, was born during a friendly discussion between a group of swimmers, cyclists and runners. The debate was simple. Who was ultimately the better athlete among them?

Well, as egos would have it, this had to be decided in the only appropriate way: *a race*. These 15 crazy athletes decided to combine three existing Honolulu-based events so they could all compete: the 2.4-mile Waikiki Roughwater Swim, the 115-mile Around Oahu Bike Race and the 26.2-mile Honolulu Marathon. The only change in the grueling course was cutting three miles off the bike course to finish at Aloha Tower. The original 15 racers took the challenge, and for what? If they finished that crazy race, they would earn the moniker of, wait for it…"IRONMAN." The race was founded by John and Judy Collins (John was a former Navy officer) and then passed on to the shepherding hands of Valerie Silk, who did a great job growing up IRONMAN in the '80s.

In 1979, *Sports Illustrated* caught wind of the race and published an article. It proved to be a game-changer in the sports world, launching IRONMAN into the public eye. That led to a coveted contract with the legendary *ABC Wide World of Sports* TV show and eventually placed the IRONMAN race and its competitors on a major media platform.

In 1988, our consortium ran across an opportunity to buy the IRONMAN, so we submitted a bid. We eventually won the bid and closed on the deal in December 1989. As part of our due diligence in buying IRONMAN, I traveled to the October 1989 IRONMAN, and man, did I time it well. October 1989 was the infamous Iron War race where IRONMAN legends Mark Allen and Dave Scott fought it out side by side to the finish. What a way to start my IRON-MAN career!

Dave Scott & Mark Allen – the Iron War race – Kona, Hawaii, 1989

My Purpose Becomes Clearer and BIGGER

Two years after we bought IRONMAN, I became the CEO. As for the race itself, you'd have to be there to understand what crossing the IRONMAN finish line means. It is more than a physical experience. Though it is quite the athletic feat, crossing that finish line fulfills a lifetime dream in one exuberant moment. It brings a supreme sense of accomplishment that is hard to match anywhere, anytime. If you can finish an IRONMAN race, what can you *not* do with the rest of your life? Simply put, the IRONMAN is the endurance world's Mount Everest.

> *"I'd watched the IRONMAN on TV for years. Staring at the screen, I cried as I watched beyond-amazing people overcome unbelievable physical challenges to cover the 140.6 windy, hot miles. The inspiration was immeasurable. I could only imagine what it must be like actually to race, and FINISH, the Hawaiian IRONMAN. And here I was. Emerging from the darkness and coming down the finishing chute with the party music blaring, the NBC TV lights shining, and the flags of the nations lining the barricades was surreal. I honestly didn't know whether to cry, laugh, or just stand there dumbfounded. It was a bit of a blur. Perhaps I did a little of all three, but my life changed at that moment. I would never doubt myself again. No. I was an IRONMAN finisher."*
>
> *~ Lincoln Murdoch* – 1997 IRONMAN Finisher*

*Note: Lincoln would later become a national triathlon champion and ministry leader, finding his own BIG LIFE.

"You are an IRONMAN!"

A competitor reaches the finish line just before the 17-hour cutoff.

Along with the purchase of IRONMAN came an *ABC Wide World of Sports* contract that helped get IRONMAN into America's living rooms. Anyone alive in the seventies will remember the famous *Wide World of Sports* broadcast with the legendary narrator, Jim McKay, opening with the phrase, "*The thrill of victory and the agony of defeat,*" when Yugoslav ski jumper Vinko Bogataj crashed and burned on the ski jump. Soon after we bought IRONMAN, the head of NBC Sports, Dick Ebersol—a.k.a. "Mr. Olympics"—offered us a privately packaged deal on NBC.

We set out with NBC to position IRONMAN as an aspirational sports brand that anyone and everyone could relate to. Even if a viewer knew they would never do the race, we wanted them to believe they could if they wanted to. I remember one meeting in Dick Ebersol's office in New York's famous 30 Rockefeller Plaza building. A few of us discussed our goal to make viewers feel as if they crossed the finish line with the athletes they saw on TV. We wanted to tell the athletes' stories in a manner that would connect with them in the same way Dick himself had pioneered with the Olympics. Over the next several years, we collaborated with some of the best at NBC Sports, including many who oversaw NBC's Olympic coverage. It was a privilege to work with the likes of Dan Hicks, Al Trautwig, Hannah Storm, Greg Lemond, and others. The experience I developed working with NBC talent would play a huge role later in my life.

Our new NBC deal gave us a two-hour show that would air twice each year, six months apart. That gave us four hours of prime NBC Sports airtime throughout the year, including healthy NBC promotion. Four hours per year might not sound like much, but that's four hours in front of millions of viewers with recorded replays and numerous network promos, so we had to do it right. We did, and soon after that, we added several ESPN shows of our International IRONMAN races. After all, it was a numbers game, and the more exposure we had, the more followers we gained. *We told our story.*

Beyond the NBC and ESPN shows, we developed and initiated a media plan in which we began telling the stories of athletes who qualified for IRONMAN in their local market. The result? We began to see our awareness skyrocket. Then it got better: our NBC show began to win Emmy Awards and numerous other accolades. We were setting the stage for a movement, and though I didn't know it at the time, the methodology and process we used to accomplish it became the building blocks for my soon-to-come tenure at Clearwater Marine Aquarium. Groundhog Day was on the way.

IRONMAN Inspirations: The Finish Line

The nighttime IRONMAN finish line. Where dreams are born.

Ah, the IRONMAN finish line!

The universe wobbles a little each October with the reverberations of inspiration that come from that small stretch of Alii Drive each October in Kona, Hawaii. The race is less about the remarkable talents of professional athletes and more about the age groupers—the average Joe and Jane's journey to the finish line.

IRONMAN is not just a sporting event. It's a lifestyle—think summiting Mt. Everest. For some, it is akin to the day their first child was born. IRONMAN is truly a life-changer: 140.6 miles of pure inspiration, perspiration and accomplishment. Crossing that finish line may mark the end of the race, but for many, it is the day they begin to *live*.

He Did What? John Maclean's Story

During my years at IRONMAN, I had a front-row seat at the finish line and witnessed many life-changing experiences, including a 70+-year-old nun (yes, a real nun) who finished the race with time to spare, proving that age really is just a state of mind. But to me, one of the most inspiring individuals to compete was an Australian named John Maclean. John had been hit by a truck in 1988 while riding his bike and became a paraplegic with very limited use of his legs. John had raced a number of triathlons and wanted to compete in IRONMAN Hawaii. In 1995, in the second year of the wheelchair event at IRONMAN Hawaii, John qualified for Kona by winning the wheelchair division in a Florida qualifying race managed by good friend Graham Fraser.

With little use of his legs, John was allowed a wetsuit to help his buoyancy for the swim. That was the only concession for wheelchair athletes. He pedaled a handcycle on the bike leg course and then used a racing wheelchair for the marathon. Okay, let's recap; this was a 140.6-mile race in devastating heat and humidity over huge hills with high-velocity winds. He participated using only his arms. Got it?

At first, nobody knew how John would do. He had to make the various interim cutoff times to continue. Racers had to finish the swim and bike segments within a certain time period. The overall finishing time allowed was 17 hours. Well, John did it all, and it was one of the most memorable feats I've ever witnessed. *Michael Jordan, move over and take a seat, please.*

The cameras were rolling as John struggled to pull his wheelchair backward with his arms up the steep hill from Kailua-Kona and onto the Queen K Highway. When the camera was on him, John flashed a grin and said, "The pain won't last forever, but the memory will." A few months after the race, John gave me the plaque below. Note the inscription:

Dave
"The Pain Won't Last Forever
But the Memory Will."
John MacLean

Anyone who has met John Maclean knows he's one of the most optimistic individuals you could ever meet. He wrote a book titled *How Far Can You Go?* which I strongly recommend. Unfortunately, countless individuals are flattened by tragedy and are unable to come back. They're trapped in the dark. Through my work at IRONMAN and later at the Clearwater Marine Aquarium, I encountered thousands of athletes and kids who could not escape the anger or the depression brought on by their life challenges, but John is the opposite. We can learn from him.

Fast-forward more than fifteen years to my new position as CEO of the Clearwater Marine Aquarium. One day my good friend and fellow former IRONMAN CEO, Lew Friedland, told me John had been recently featured on *60 Minutes Australia* and was learning to walk again. What? That was unthinkable and out of the question back when I knew John.

Shortly after that, John visited Clearwater Marine Aquarium, and that's when I experienced one of life's few truly indescribable moments. I turned the corner to meet John, and here he was walking toward me! I almost dropped to my knees in awe to see him standing on both legs without outside support. But John is the kind of guy who refuses to give up, so he fought through his problem and, with a commitment to a non-conventional therapy (and with the aid of carbon fiber leg braces), miraculously found a way to walk again.

John reminded me of Winter the dolphin's story, so I wanted them to meet. Winter lost her tail and had little chance of surviving. We were advised to euthanize her the night she arrived, but we refused. With some help, Winter found ways to overcome her obstacles and emerged victoriously. More on her story later. There I was with two miracles from the two big chapters in my life—John, the IRONMAN miracle, and Winter, the dolphin miracle—together at the same time. At that moment, the world was good. That experience reinforced my life purpose: to bring hope and life-changing inspiration to as many as possible.

Two miracles meet

Another Crawl of Fame:
The Wendy Ingraham and Sian Welch Story

As I noted earlier, IRONMAN came to fame with that infamous crawl to the finish line in the 1982 race. I was not at that race, but I was about to experience another IRONMAN "crawl of fame." In 1997, Wendy Ingraham and Sian Welch—top professional female triathletes—raced all 140.6 miles upright, except for the last few feet. As they struggled toward the finish line, they both collapsed about 75 feet before the line. Not kidding.

I can still hear the voice of longtime legendary IRONMAN race announcer Mike Reilly calling it out. After nine-plus hours of racing, while actually in the finish line chute, their minds got ahead of their bodies, and they shut down and collapsed. Sian and Wendy wobbled and fell at the same time. These are the moments in life where the world stops, and you feel like you're in a dream. So what would a couple of real fighters do? They would get to the finish line at any cost and do whatever it takes because it's about finishing the job. They would crawl if they had to. And that's exactly what they did! They crawled. Nothing but hands and knees for every agonizing foot until they crossed the line. It was one of the most memorable finishes of any race, ever. You can find the crazy and inspiring video on YouTube.

Wendy Ingraham & Sian Welch – 1997 IRONMAN

IRONMAN is about having the will and tenacity to train when no one is watching and finishing the race under your own power. The parallel message is clear; a willingness to *swim upstream* together with an overcoming, never-say-die attitude is what both IRONMAN and Winter the dolphin are all about. Those who finish IRONMAN excel at life because IRONMAN builds and reflects character, perseverance, and confidence. That is precisely what happens with the kids and wounded soldiers who connect with Winter's overcoming story. Those who finish an IRONMAN may walk away with a medal, but more importantly, they leave with a renewed life and purpose. Those who connected with Winter the dolphin experienced the same thing. Life is about overcoming and achieving. Winter's story is coming up soon.

Is there a finish line in your life you need to cross? A dream you had years ago that you gave up on, something you started but never finished? Pick up your dream and move forward. It's time. And take God with you; it's an easier trip.

An IRONMAN Lottery of Hope

Bob Jordan was an upper-echelon FBI agent who had the crazy dream of doing the IRONMAN race in Hawaii. It wasn't so crazy, though, because Bob had a big reason: his beautiful five-year-old daughter, Emily, had cancer, and her prognosis had worsened. Bob's good intentions aside, however, IRONMAN is extremely competitive, and only a handful of slots were available on a lottery basis for the 1997 race.

Little Emily had been asking Dad what he wanted for his upcoming birthday. Of course, his answer was always, "For you to get well and come home with us, Emily." But that wasn't enough for her. "I know, Dad, but what gift do you want?" she asked. "Well," he replied, "you know I'd love to get into the IRONMAN race." Those words, spoken to a child, would set off a chain of events not soon forgotten. Not long after that conversation, this letter showed up on my desk:

Emily Jordan
13184 Ireland Lane
San Diego CA 92129

Hospital Address: Room 323
UCLA Medical Center
10833 Le Conte Ave
LA CA 90095

April 9, 1997

Dear Lottery People
   My name is Emily. I am 5 years old. My dad's name
is Bob. He is a triathlete. Please pick him for the Ironman.

   I have trained with my dad every week since I was 3 weeks old,
either sitting in the jogger or riding in the bike trailer. Now,
my little brother Timothy goes with Dad because I am in
the hospital. My brother is 3 months old today.

   I am having a bone marrow transplant to get rid of
my leukemia. My dad's birthday is in 2 weeks but I can't
leave my isolation room to get him a present. Maybe, if I write
a letter you will pick him for the Ironman?

   When I asked my dad, "What do you want for your birthday?"
he said, "I want you to be healed, Emily!" I said, "Okay, what else
do you want?" He said, "To complete the Ironman in Hawaii and to
have you, Mommy and Timothy at the finish line!" Please pick my dad.

   If you pick my dad, you will make a great choice. He will be
smiling the whole day of the race because it would be his big
dream come true! He has applied every year since before I was
even born. This is his 10th try. Please pick my dad.

   He has finished 2 Ironman-distance races and I helped him
with hugs, water and a little massage. Please pick my dad! But,
if you don't, he is still an Ironman to me. Thank you!
                                    Love,
P.S. My mom helped me with this
letter. Don't tell my dad.   (Emily)
          It's a surprise!

46

"Please pick my Dad." Wow. I'll never forget that letter. The decision was quick. I would put her dad in the race. Up to that point, I had given complimentary slots to the likes of Governor Jerry Johnson of New Mexico, David Nordstrom (yes, the Nordstrom store guy), Alexandra Paul, the former *Baywatch* TV show star, and NFL player Darryl Haley. Obviously, the lottery attracted star power for IRONMAN marketing purposes, but what heartless fool would turn down little Emily's request? My daughter, Tiffany, was nearly the same age as Emily, which made the letter even more personal to me.

It was a no-brainer. The dad in me said yes, so I talked it over with my staff, and we decided to do Emily one better. Working with Terry (Emily's mom), we planned to surprise Bob with his invitation in a creative way, but we needed to move quickly. Emily was hospitalized and was very sick, so we arranged for cameras from the TV show *Inside Edition* to film Bob discovering he was invited to do IRONMAN on behalf of Emily. Here is Bob in his own words:

> *"Emily's transplant failed, and she was in great pain fighting the intubation. The doctors recommended an induced coma while they did a global search for another bone marrow match. We agreed to that reality as we had no other choice, and she was in that coma starting around April 20th.*
>
> *My birthday is April 24th, the day Inside Edition came to the UCLA Medical Center. While still in the coma, they moved her out of her room, and I sat with her in the ICU. Then Terry summoned me to Emily's old room for what was supposed to be my birthday 'party.' Some of my San Diego FBI Squad mates had driven up to LA for the occasion, although we all understood there was not much to celebrate. I guess everyone but me knew about the gift of the slot.*
>
> *After everybody left, Terry and I went down to Emily's room to sit with her and tell her the slot had come. That was the closest I got to thank her. They never found a donor match, and we had to let her go. She never came out of that coma.*
>
> *We lost her on the 29th."*

In one of the most heroic performances I ever witnessed, Bob, with a heavy heart and the support of thousands, made the pilgrimage to Kona that year and fought all day and crossed the hallowed IRONMAN finish line in honor of his little girl.

As I write this, I still struggle with the emotions this story brings up. Everyone knew about Emily's condition; we knew this was far more than just getting a guy into our race. It was about honoring a dying five-year-old daughter. In addition to the compassion I felt for them, I was overcome with gratefulness that I could have something to do with bringing a blessing to a hurting family when they needed it. Being CEO of IRONMAN wasn't a job … it was a gift from God.

I got to know Bob and Terry that year and was amazed at how well they handled the situation. It was a scenario that I doubt I could have endured myself. They were a class act, and they inspired millions as they allowed us to tell their story on NBC.

Twenty years later, Bob sent me this post on Facebook.

> "Hi, David, Terry, and I and our 9-month-old son Timothy were on the BIG Island for the IRONMAN event. It was my first time, and I know you remember how my daughter, Emily, and IRONMAN got me there. After the race, you met the three of us in the transition area, and after you saw me, you gave Terry the key to your room at the King Kamehameha Hotel and told us to take as long as we needed to rest. We've all come a long way since then, but thank you again for that kindness."

Little Emily, in her few short years, found a way to live a BIG LIFE. She spent her final days trying to help someone close to her … Dad. The number of years we live doesn't determine our success in life; it's how we use the years God gives us. That is a life lesson from little Emily. Twenty-two years later, Bob qualified for the 2019 IRONMAN and is now a top-rated age-group triathlete.

Go, Bob! You are an IRONMAN, in every sense of the word.

Bob & Emily

Saving Time-X

"Time, time, time is on my side, yes it is ..."
~ The Rolling Stones

I love the song, but Mick, that's just not true. Time *is* fleeting, brother.

I'm a big believer in using time wisely as we have limited time to fulfill our God-given purpose. You don't know how much time you have on this earth. That's why I encourage you not to waste it. I try to be a fast mover to save time. Now at IRONMAN, we had a chance to help save—wait for it— *Timex!* Say what?

We had a relationship with Timex that was critical for us at the time. They sold a watch using our IRONMAN name and paid us a royalty for each watch sold. It kept the company in the black, and without it, we would have struggled. In 1992, Timex informed me they were about to launch a new night lighting system on their watches. It was called Indiglo. They said it would be revolutionary and stressed that they were willing to launch it on the IRONMAN watch but wanted a better royalty arrangement.

It was clear that Timex wanted to launch it with the IRONMAN watch because of its skyrocketing popularity. I recognized this was a critical juncture in IRONMAN's life. If I handled it right, we stood to gain on two fronts. First, we would increase our revenues, and second, the success of the product could drive other licensing deals our way in the future.

After a couple of months of negotiations, we settled on a long-term arrangement that gave Timex long-term options. We negotiated a different deal where the more IRONMAN watches they sold, the less percentage they would have to pay incrementally. That gave them an additional incentive to push our watches. It was a classic win-win. They were happy, and we were delighted. Eventually, the Timex IRONMAN watch became the best-selling line in the US and possibly the world. Tens of millions of those watches were sold, and since the product line continues to this day, it's likely many of you have had an IRONMAN watch on your wrist.

The key to our dealings with Timex was for us not to be greedy but to have a long-game view of the relationship. It gave Timex room to expand the IRONMAN watch line with multiple new designs and technologies. That strategy paid off in spades for everyone. In later conversations with their executives, we found out that Timex's sports watch line, led by the IRONMAN watch, literally saved their company when it ran into financial trouble in the early nineties.

You might say the IRONMAN watch saved both companies.

"Unlike sport, in business, the win-win is the best possible score."

~ Rasheed Ogunlaru

IRONMAN Meets Iron Man

As time rolls along, we realize that life is full of big junctures punctuated with pivotal moments. I was blessed to have more than my share of them. My dealings with Timex stood at one of those junctures. Another one that popped up around the same time had to do with—wait for it—a comic book. The previous IRONMAN owner had signed a "trademark coexistence" agreement with Marvel Comics (yes, *that* Marvel Comics, the Stan Lee guy company). As you probably know, Marvel has its own Iron Man character that predates the IRONMAN Triathlon.

Although Marvel's Iron Man and our IRONMAN were vastly different brands reaching different demographics, Marvel claimed that it still had the legal upper hand. Our predecessor had agreed to terms that limited our use of the IRONMAN brand in numerous ways. If we were to pursue the full brand potential we envisioned without violating the contract, we wanted to get the contract restrictions loosened substantially.

After we purchased IRONMAN, we went to work and called for a meeting with Marvel Comics to discuss these issues. That first meeting was a doozy. It was "Iron Man meets IRONMAN" in the boardroom. To put it into context, this was 1990, about the time when Timex IRONMAN watch sales had begun to skyrocket. The meeting took place in the office of their law firm in Manhattan with a direct view of the Statue of Liberty. You can't get any more American than that. Here's what happened:

We strolled into the vast conference room and found half a dozen of their people waiting for us, including executives, attorneys, and other top brass. The scent of war was palpable. During their opening salvo, one of the Marvel team tossed an IRONMAN watch across the table to us and commented on the IRONMAN name inscribed on it. Let's just say that set the tone.

What followed was the New York corporate world version of a food fight. When they finished pushing, we pushed back. Then they pushed again, and we pushed right back. And so on. I kept thinking, *Here I am looking out the window at the revered Statue of Liberty, the symbol of freedom and unity, while we're in the middle of a hardcore business shouting match. Spider-Man, take me away!* Marvel knew we needed them to lift some of the restrictions, but we told them we could make millions with the restrictions as they stood, and they would get nothing from it. We made it clear that if they would negotiate and modify their conditions, they could secure part of the action as we grew the brand. It was a long meeting, heavy on posturing, with multiple breaks for each side to reassess their position.

As the sun set over lower Manhattan, the meeting ended in a stalemate. We parted with the understanding that we would keep talking. To follow up, Marvel assigned a short, middle-aged guy named Joe Calamari as their contact. His nickname was Joe "The Squid" Calamari (not making this up). Joe was quite a character who dressed and spoke with as much color and spunk as his name implied. He wore bright suspenders and had a classic flamboyant New York personality. I say this with respect, as he was a great guy. During our ongoing negotiations, Joe kept throwing out that they were in the process of developing an Iron Man movie and didn't want to give up any intellectual property rights. He even dropped Steven Spielberg's name as a possible movie partner.

Now mind you, this all happened well before the Marvel movie franchise we all know and love came to be. It was also a time when Marvel was reportedly close to bankruptcy, so when Joe brought up their movie aspirations, we politely mocked him with, "Oh sure, Joe. Can I buy the first ticket?" It was all in good fun, but we still pushed back mercilessly.

Eventually, we developed great relationships with the Marvel team, and working with them was one of the highlights of my career. It would take a couple of years of biding my time, but once they were on the verge of bankruptcy—and I thought I had the right resources and environment to make a new win-win deal—I approached them again. This time I was able to negotiate additional rights to our benefit, and in the end, both brands won. Win-win was the goal in the first place. It just took time to get there.

The broadening of our rights for our IRONMAN name would be a critical factor in our company's growth, and there's a lesson in all this. When you hit a mountain in a business deal or a personal relationship and find yourself at a standstill, look for the win-win. Ask yourself what the other side needs for them to come to terms.

Oh, as a footnote to the whole affair, fifteen years later, Marvel had a bit of success with a little Iron Man movie series you may have heard of. It starred some guy named Robert Downey, Jr., I think.

Swimming Upstream – The Federations

Before and during my IRONMAN years, the sport of triathlon was under consideration to be recognized as an Olympic sport. The process was long, drawn-out, and highly political. To attain the status as an Olympic sport, its organizers first have to develop a federation system. That means establishing an international governing body to provide the sport with regulatory and sanctioning functions, among other things. Then, every country must have its own *national* federation that reports to the *international* federation. Further, each sport has to be "participatory," meaning a minimum number of countries must have the sport active in their country. Finally, the "sport" gets to a vote. It is this last part that makes the federations highly political. Like any election, whoever gets the most votes gets their sport in the Olympic Games.

That was the current process being played out in the sport of triathlon at the time; that is, until I came on the scene. Our IRONMAN Triathlon franchise, our logo, and our marketing message rocked many boats in the Olympic Federation community. We got in the way of more than a few federation issues, since the federations were required to maintain certain controls over their particular sport. In our case, the popularity of the IRONMAN events transcended the sport of triathlon. The public knew us far better than any other triathlon event, or the entire sport for that matter. Further, we had a more significant TV package for IRONMAN than even the Boston or New York City Marathons, even though running was, and always will be, a much larger participatory sport than triathlon.

The real conflict stemmed from our use of the IRONMAN "World Championship" name. The international federation (not the US federation which I got along fine with) wanted to control the use of that phrase; they considered "World Championship" part of their bailiwick. On one level, it made sense: if everyone claimed to run a "World Championship" event, confusion would reign. I get that.

On the other hand, our company predated the international federation's control because we had used the "World Championship" moniker for years. We had assigned "World Championship" to our IRONMAN Hawaii event and had already held numerous IRONMAN qualifying events worldwide that fed into it. As we became more successful, our reach broadened, and the federation had little control over us. They didn't like it, and I didn't care because we held the trademark and were not about to give it up.

This was the scenario when I joined IRONMAN, and over time the animosity between the international federation and me grew. I earned the reputation as the one leading the charge, not against the Olympics, but the international federation and their requirements. I saw their dealings as power plays.

Then in 1996, something very odd happened: I was invited by the international federation president to attend their annual congress in Cancun, Mexico. In a personal note to me, he said he wanted to discuss our differences. That was all fine and good until we attempted to enter the congress hall for the first meeting, and they barred us from entering. There was no reason and no explanation given, but as a former union leader, well, it was not surprising. Unions play hardball. Apparently, barring me from the meeting he had personally invited me to was just the way he rolled. It also showed me the truly political nature of the federation movement.

After many years of federation pushback on our legitimate business, I'd had enough. I dropped an H-bomb in the middle of their world by filing an antitrust lawsuit against the international federation. Our action caught the attention of the IOC (International Olympic Committee). As far as I know, it was the first-ever such lawsuit, largely because in the world of Olympic sports, one didn't dare take on the powerful federations for risk of being blackballed from the sport altogether. The lawsuit was still in place when I left IRONMAN.

Despite all of this, I always was, and still am, a fan of the actual Olympic Games and watch them wholeheartedly. This was a conflict between myself and one person and should not reflect on the entire federation system. There are great people in the system, and the Olympic movement is needed more today than ever. Ironically, a friend I knew was in charge of the Olympic Torch Relay back in the nineties. With his help, the kids and I carried the torch in the 1996 Atlanta Games relay as it passed through Florida.

Jordan, Tiffany, Chris and Josh out for an Olympic Torch jog with Dad

My time with IRONMAN was filled with a variety of both amazing and difficult situations. Beyond the federation issues, I was one of the people leading the charge against PEDs (performance-enhancing drugs) in our sport. One year the winner of the IRONMAN was alleged to have used EPO (blood doping), and it became a big controversy, which almost put our NBC TV show at risk for that year. Another year my race director and I had our lives threatened by an anonymous call to the IRONMAN race office and had to have police protection the rest of that week. We didn't let this threat stop us. The point is that your life will have challenges; it's what you do with them that matters.

In the end, the IRONMAN Triathlon is a journey of perseverance, courage, endurance and getting to the finish line. Like those who have finished the race, I know the power of life-changing inspiration. Who could have guessed that a decade later, a rescued dolphin would come into my life, her story rivaling IRONMAN's symbol of inspiration and courage? Or that my journey with Winter the dolphin and her unique story would so closely mirror my journey with IRONMAN? I guess that makes me a fan of Groundhog Day. Good things often repeat themselves.

5

THE VALLEY

Of all people, you would think the CEO of IRONMAN would know how to pace himself. Well, sorry, I did not. I had run hard, and nearly everything I had learned was OJT (on-the-job training), a fairly stressful way to learn the CEO role. Remember the IRONMAN stories I mentioned where runners collapse just before they get to the finish line? That was kinda where I was in my life. It was like I was so intent on swimming upstream that I completely forgot to come up for air, and I was drowning myself. I had ignored the signs of stress and anxiety and had caught myself routinely dreaming of the day I stepped down. I should have observed the telltale signs and taken a break, but no, I just kept pushing ahead. *No cup of Gatorade or energy bar could save me.* After nearly ten years of high-speed running with the company, I ran out of gas. I was burnt to a crisp, mentally and emotionally fried. So I quit. Just like that. I turned in my keys and sold my stock back to the other owners. I didn't leave the organization the way I should have. It was very abrupt. Everyone was surprised, to say the very least. Many thought I was sick. Some in the media guessed I had cancer or some other disease. Actually, I had the condition famously known as "burnout." I just desperately needed a break. I was only 38, but with four young kids, I was also tired of missing too many baseball games, basketball games and gymnastics routines.

A Gymnasium Epiphany

Looking back, I realized my IRONMAN "run" was nearing completion a year or so before—it had been another epiphany in my life. We were visiting my wife's family in rural western Nebraska, where we attended a local high school basketball game. It was small-town life at its best. During halftime, a guy came out to sweep the gym floor. As I sipped my Coke, I watched him methodically go from one end of the floor to another, pushing his wide broom. I was mesmerized, almost coveting his apparent low-key, stress-free life, and I found myself yearning to run onto the floor to help him. Give me the broom! I felt like I was in the middle of the movie *Hoosiers,* a great film about a small-town Indiana basketball team. That should have been a wake-up call to me, but like most Type A's, a yellow light means hit the gas rather than slow down. That is until you crash, as I did.

Now that my career was on hold, I found myself with too much time on my hands. I still had a lot to learn, but at least this one huge lesson in my life had been hard-won:

Working hard and playing hard is fine as long as you know how to pace yourself. Don't let youthful zealousness and good intentions cause your career and life to crash. An out-of-balance life cannot be sustained. Your BIG LIFE requires you to be around to do it. Just sayin' …

My leaving IRONMAN shook everyone, including my wife, who wanted to kill me for quitting without a plan. She was right: leaving the company so abruptly wasn't ideal. I had to repair some relationships later on. It's hard to make the right decisions when your vision is clouded like mine was.

And so, leaving IRONMAN was the beginning of an eight-year journey in which there were very few mountaintops in a seemingly endless valley. To put it mildly, it was a *long* eight years. There was an initial upside, though; now that I was free of the constant grind of corporate life, I spent more time with my family. (Although I think after a few months, Joan was like: "Uh, honey, I love you, but you can go do something now." Translation: *Get out of the house, honey.*)

Once I was rested, I looked around for ways I could use my business experience. For a while, I bought and sold small company stocks, consulted for a few small businesses, and managed my own funds. All of that kept me busy, but my overarching need was to find a renewed purpose for my life. I was miserable, so it couldn't come too quickly.

Most people have a misunderstanding that successful people have nothing but wins. That is entirely untrue. As I said earlier, some of our best life lessons come from our failures, and I had plenty. The key is to LEARN from them and not repeat them.

> "I've missed more than 9,000 shots in my career. I've lost almost 300
> games. 26 times I've been trusted to take the game-winning shot and
> missed. I've failed over and over and over again in my life,
> and that is why I succeed."
>
> ~ Michael Jordan

IRONMAN was in my rearview mirror now, and I needed a new mountain to summit. True to form, my life was about to take one of those unexpected turns I've talked about. Having been inspired by the hundreds of overcomers I met during my time at IRONMAN, I connected with several faith-based and humanitarian ministries. One of them led me to Vietnam to help persecuted minorities.

Finding Purpose in My Valley: A Time to Help Others

A few years earlier, I had met one of the great mentors in my life, a very successful man named Ray, who introduced me to a man who founded a nonprofit organization assisting Vietnam's needy. This man—we'll call him John for security reasons—was a former officer in the South Vietnamese Army. After Saigon's fall, he fled the country before being assigned to a "re-education camp," a sanitized name for a death sentence for many.

John managed to buy a boat and make his escape. In the process, he fled with 88 orphans and a few adults. They shipped out on the South China Sea with no idea where they would end up or even if they would survive the trip. Worse yet, he had hired a boat captain who turned out to be anything but that as he had lied about his experience just to escape Vietnam. The group drifted aimlessly on the sea for days until a US ship found them and towed their boat to Singapore, nearly capsizing it many times on the dangerous trip. If they tipped, they would all surely drown. They survived the journey, found refuge in an American military base there, then immigrated to the US to start a new life. In the early '90s, John returned to Vietnam, where he began conducting faith-based and humanitarian work in coordination with hundreds of small "house churches." The Vietnamese government is not always fond of this kind of assistance to their people, so he had to work in secret throughout the years, often fleeing to avoid arrest. John's work in Vietnam appealed to me, so I volunteered to help out with my skill set.

I flew to Vietnam twice, once in 2001 for one week and then later in 2004 for two and a half weeks. As I traveled around the country with John, I felt the heavy air of profound poverty and government oppression. We met in secret with the wives of a couple of dozen wrongfully imprisoned pastors. In the emotionally charged encounter, they poured out their hearts, telling us how the police had whisked their husbands away in the middle of the night to one of their notoriously overcrowded prisons. No cable TV or pool tables there. Their crime? Operating a church and helping people. How dare they.

We had scheduled another meeting in Hanoi at a hotel but had to switch locations when we heard the police were aware of us. In that meeting, we met the wife of a pastor killed for his humanitarian and church work. At the same meeting, another man had just been released from prison but seemed very distant and disconnected. When I asked John what happened to the man, he told me about the horrific way they torture the prisoners and that many never mentally recover.

John is holding the hand of a man who is a blind, leprous villager in front of a freshwater well we dug. This person is rarely touched and, by doing so, it shows great respect for the man.

Orphans sleeping on the floor in an orphanage we support

"Every storm runs out of rain just like every dark night turns into day."

~ Gary Allan

Another Chance to Help

In 2012, I was introduced to another man who oversaw a similar faith-based humanitarian effort in Pakistan. He wanted me to get involved, but before I did, I needed to see the work in Pakistan firsthand like I did with the ministry in Vietnam. So I went, and man, was that an ordeal! The "Arab Spring" uprising was in full swing, with many Islamic countries enduring great unrest, including Pakistan. I signed in on the US State Department website to let them know of my travel plans. Almost immediately, I received a slew of "travel advisories" as to why I should *not* visit Pakistan. I read them with interest but decided to go anyway. That was in January of 2013.

After a long day and a half of travel, I arrived in Islamabad around 2:00 a.m. one morning. When I emerged from the plane and turned my phone on, I immediately saw an alarming news alert from the State Department. They were suddenly directing US citizens not to travel to Pakistan, informing us that the US Embassy would shut down. Wait, what? Seriously? I just landed.

Now, not all Pakistanis are entirely welcoming to Americans. Add to that, while I was in Pakistan, the movie *Zero Dark Thirty* was released. The movie was about the killing of Osama Bin Laden, and the compound where he was killed was about an hour from where I was staying. Yikes. As if that weren't enough, a political coup attempt was also in process on live TV, and the government shut down the airport while I was there. I couldn't begin to make all of this up.

Nevertheless, as crazy as it was, it was all for a good reason. Before I could get involved in assisting these people, I had to experience how they lived. Well, I experienced it all in a very intense five days!

When I talk about living a BIG LIFE, it doesn't mean we all have to run a major company or produce movies. If that's what you do, great, but living a big life can mean just about anything. These people in Vietnam and Pakistan, many of them impoverished and broken, are living their own BIG LIVES in a way that humbles me. It's about making an impact with your life wherever God places you and not missing the opportunity to do that. Proverbs 3:3 says: "Let love and faithfulness never leave you; bind them around your neck, write them on the tablet of your heart." The point: kindness toward others always leads you to a BIG LIFE.

Over the years, our work in Vietnam and Pakistan has helped tens of thousands of poverty-stricken people. It has provided economic assistance, taught hundreds of adults of low socioeconomic status new trades, dug innumerable freshwater wells in impoverished areas, and supported hundreds of homeless orphan street children. It has also brought numerous children out of the Cambodian sex trade and helped hundreds of rural churches get on their feet and assist their communities. The work continues to this day, and as of this writing, we have raised millions of dollars for these projects. The men and women who do this work live the ultimate BIG LIVES through selfless service while living on a meager income. You don't know their names, but God does. Their BIG LIVES trounce anything I could ever do. I simply used my time and skill sets to assist the amazing men and women already involved in the work.

Remember, you only have one life, so what will your legacy be? Are you in the valley right now? If so, look up! There's plenty of work to be done. Living a BIG LIFE means looking for opportunities to serve while in your own personal valley. Living a BIG LIFE doesn't stop due to hardship; it continues despite the hardship. It may feel like you're swimming upstream. And if you are, that's okay! Just keep swimming.

David & Kids in Rawalpindi, Pakistan (near Islamabad)

A Hard Reality

Although I enjoyed assisting John and others in Vietnam and Pakistan, my own financial valley was about to get even more profound. While my pro-bono nonprofit work was personally satisfying and helped others, I eventually ran into a financial buzz saw. It turned out that a few friends who worked for a Tampa-based nonprofit ministry we supported inadvertently walked me into a financial "investment" that was nothing short of a fraud. That rocked my world and sent me into a few very cash-strapped years. Believe it or not, the "investment" included involvement with a man who is now a sitting judge in Georgia. That led me to spend a lot of time over the last twenty years working to expose government corruption in Georgia. On any given weekend, you can still find me filming corrupt junkets undercover with well-known media outlets or submitting information on scam rings to the FBI.

Several people who owed me a lot of money were not paying, so I had to litigate. That, of course, cost more money. Although I won large judgments against seven of them, I still had to collect the funds myself. Unfortunately, the courts don't do that for you.

The situation dragged on for months and then years. During that time, we sold our house, cut back on our lifestyle, and basically just fell off a cliff financially. I also ran out of things to do but knew I had to do something. *Anything.*

So one day, I walked a few blocks to our local post office and pleaded with them: "Just keep me busy, please." You heard me right; the former IRONMAN CEO was now working at the post office to maintain his sanity. How's that for an oxymoron?

You can bet I got some funny looks from a few postal employees who knew who I was. I became good friends with a number of them and respected their hard work. There weren't any part-time or temporary CEO roles out there, so this is what I did to keep busy while I continued to reclaim what was owed me and figure out what would be my next career move. Joan and I had considered moving out of the area for some possible executive career positions, but we didn't want to rip our kids from the only life they knew, like what happened to me when we moved from Iowa to Texas. I knew that feeling.

So that was my valley, and I kept slogging through it. I was disoriented, frustrated, wondering what in the heck I was doing. How could I go from running a global sports company to working as a newbie at the post office or Domino's? I felt my purpose in life had come to a screeching halt. This entire ordeal since I left IRONMAN didn't last for weeks; it lasted eight long *years*. Yet time often brings with it a different perspective, and because "hindsight is 20/20," I now know this extremely difficult season was precisely what I needed. I found hope and purpose by helping others while I waited for my own life to turn around. I had risen and fallen about as far as you can in a short period of time, but a fantastic turnaround was just ahead. It would be another Kilimanjaro experience: I couldn't see it, but God could. While I was wandering around in the desert, He was planning.

"Every champion was once a contender that didn't give up."

~ Gabby Douglas

6

NEW HORIZONS: FINDING RENEWED PURPOSE

"I've got to take chances and get out there. What are you going to do, sit home and knit? I don't knit."

~ Cybill Shepherd

Humble Beginnings

In late 2005, my wife, Joan, heard that Clearwater Marine Aquarium (CMA) was looking for a CEO. I didn't take it too seriously as I wanted to find a larger organization to lead, something of the magnitude of IRONMAN. At that point, all I knew about CMA was that it had a small town "mom and pop" feel to it. Old school, laid back, not exactly modern, but with a cool mission. For some reason, the position intrigued me. They were in severe financial trouble (and I like to fix things), so I threw my hat in the ring. What the heck, why not?

In January of 2006, I was offered the position of CEO. After eight years of wandering from one hardship to another, I finally land at a financially strapped nonprofit that's ready to close? What was I thinking? Although the job was mine, I had to get beyond the blur of insolvency and find a vision. What was my purpose here? At IRONMAN, I oversaw a company that inspired millions worldwide, but CMA seemed like a really small purpose to the naked eye. Not just small, but an itsy-bitsy teeny-weeny purpose. But there I was.

Fair enough.

I took a chance when I stayed with IRONMAN instead of going back into the CPA profession. I guess I could do the same thing with a rundown education and marine life rescue center, right? To anyone looking from the outside, the odds of turning CMA around so it could survive, much less succeed, were slim to none (and slim had just Ubered out of town!). That swimming upstream thing was about to be tested big time. But I was upbeat and expectant. After all, as the saying goes, if you don't take the first step, you go nowhere.

The Origin of Clearwater Marine Aquarium

Clearwater Marine Aquarium originated as an idea, a dream, in 1972. A few years later, the City of Clearwater donated a sewage treatment plant to a visionary professor/scientist, Heyward Matthews, and CMA's first executive director, Dennis Kellenberger, who both wanted to convert the plant into an environmental education facility. Originally named the Clearwater Marine Science Center (after intensive cleaning with buckets of Lysol!), the facility opened its doors in 1979 as a nonprofit organization focused mainly on marine-based education. Years later, they added *marine life rescue* as part of the mission to facilitate their educational goals.

Clearwater Water Treatment Facility – 1970s

The organization soon ran into a marketing challenge: the public didn't seem to understand they could visit the facility. To attract more visitors, they replaced "Science Center" with the word "Aquarium." That step made sense at the time because their support came mainly from visitor gate revenues. More visitors meant more revenue, which was important because rescued animals don't have Obamacare, Medicare, or any other insurance, plus their rescue, care and feeding are quite expensive. Look at it this way: Helping distressed marine life is the ultimate example of helping those who can do absolutely nothing in return. CMA guests help pay for this work by buying a ticket while getting an inspiring and educational experience.

Sea turtle release – Clearwater Beach

When I was hired, CMA was just months away from closing down, so marching order #1 was to try and keep CMA alive. Being a man of the '70s and in true allegiance to the Bee Gees, my daily challenge was "staying alive, staying alive." I swear I heard that dang song in my head every day. Just stay alive, stay alive. I was told the organization was on fire, but that analogy was comparable to saying a tsunami is coming, so expect moisture! Financially, CMA was falling off a cliff, and everything about the facility was going up in flames. The main building was close to being condemned, we were in violation of dozens of agency oversight rules, and any animal care equipment we had was dilapidated. You might say our animal life support systems were on life support.

Our staff of 35 was dispirited and fractured, and our volunteers had fled like a back-door revival. Most of the donor base had packed up and hightailed it out of there long before. Just days after I started, my team informed me the roof above the main dolphin pool could cave in at any moment. Excuse me, would you repeat that? Yep, cave right in. And if it did, people and animals would die—that kind of cave-in.

Other than that, Clearwater Marine Aquarium was in great shape.

Spinner Dolphin Rescue – 2017

I felt like the captain of the *Titanic*—*after* it hit the iceberg. What the heck was I thinking? Did I just make a huge career mistake? CMA was failing, and if I couldn't save it, how would that impact the rest of my career? I was okay with swimming upstream but not drowning upstream! I could do everything right, and it could still fail, considering the condition it was in. But I had taken the job, so off I went.

It was time to solve problems, set a vision, and try to save this little treasure at Clearwater Beach. Who would guess that this small, 50,000-square-foot former sewage plant would reach around the world and inspire millions in nearly every country? Who would imagine it would become a mecca of life-changing inspiration? Who would think that on any given day, numerous families would arrive, having made a pilgrimage from the four corners of the earth to meet a little dolphin their child had clung to while struggling through a dark season in their life?

I did. In fact, that's the kind of stuff I dream about all day long.

The point: It takes one person to start a movement. Look at every great movement in society. One person had to see it and act on it.

But I had a long way to go to build this vision. My immediate thoughts were on the roof, as I had no desire to die that way. While my first job was to save CMA, there was something else brewing that I was unaware of when I started … something of great significance that some had overlooked.

Facebook Live releasing a rehabilitated seahorse. Yes, a seahorse.
We actually did that. Check it out at SeeWinter.com.

"Dreams don't work unless you do."

~ John Maxwell

Flashback to December 10, 2005

A few weeks before I started as CEO, the Clearwater Marine Aquarium team carried out their duties like most any other day. Around 3:00 p.m., a call came in about a baby dolphin being rescued on the other side of the state. It was a cold Saturday afternoon. Okay, so maybe cold is an overstatement, but we're Floridians. So, maybe it was a bone-chilling 60°. A local fisherman named Jim Savage discovered a baby dolphin entangled in a crab trap rope. The dolphin was in an area called Mosquito Lagoon—an appropriate name if you've ever been there (think massive mosquitoes). It's near Cape Canaveral on the Florida Space Coast. The dolphin appeared to be severely stressed. Savage realized he had to move quickly, as her only chance of survival was to make it to a marine animal hospital. His phone call would be one for the record books.

The government oversight agency made several calls to nearby facilities; we were the only available one, and we were four hours away. One of our partner teams took over the rescue and eventually loaded the seriously injured dolphin into what we call a "stranding van." They headed to Clearwater, and, upon arrival, our team members took over, swiftly transporting the female bottlenose dolphin on a stretcher into CMA. It was touch and go.

While Winter fought to live, nearly everyone in our industry advised us to euthanize her. "Put her down," they urged. To be fair, this was an understandable suggestion as calamities like this don't usually end well for young dolphins. But we said no, and, as it turns out, this might be one of the best decisions in wildlife rescue history.

We maintained a 24-hour watch over Winter with our staff and volunteers pulling four-hour shifts. Most of them felt when they ended their shift that it would be the last time they would see her. Winter had massive external injuries and had suffered severe dehydration along with other maladies. We kinda knew how these things go, so we were afraid this wasn't going to end well.

After a few days, we produced a formal summary of the newly rescued dolphin's condition. That was standard procedure for all rescues. The following are actual notes from Winter's case file:

> *Upon arrival at CMA, Winter's condition was regarded as critical, with the prevailing prognosis being an unfavorable outcome based on what we knew about stranded marine mammals and comparisons to historical cetacean rehabilitation cases. She was further compromised as an orphaned calf still dependent on her mother for survival, as well as other compounding variables associated with age, stress, nutrition, and a weakened immune response.*

And then, the most significant part of her injuries:

> *It was apparent Winter suffered significant trauma to the distal portion of her peduncle and tail flukes, including penetrating wounds due to a rope entanglement that had wrapped tightly around the circumference of the peduncle. An evaluation of Winter's movements in the water revealed the disabling nature of the injury, although the*

extent of it was unknown and later discovered after a more thorough clinical evaluation.

Translation: *Winter was critical.*

Taking all these conditions into account, the overall prognosis for Winter's survival was "not favorable," and that was a glass-half-full way of looking at it. Her tail flukes had been severely damaged due to the blood flow being cut off by the tightly wound ropes around her tail base area known as the peduncle. There was no way she could swim if she lost her tail flukes, or so we thought.

The Vigil

Winter was rescued on December 10, 2005, and our team named her Winter because of that date. A little-known secret is that we later realized that date was not technically the winter season yet. However, I wasn't about to switch her name to Fall, so we stuck with Winter! By the time I started at CMA, Winter had lost her entire tail (both tail flukes) and two of her vertebrae. Contrary to popular belief, we did not perform a one-time amputation; instead, we performed a daily procedure called "debriding" that required cutting off the dead tissue until it was finally gone. The result was a baby dolphin with a variety of potentially deadly medical issues and no tail flukes. Her incredibly small odds of survival had shrunk even further.

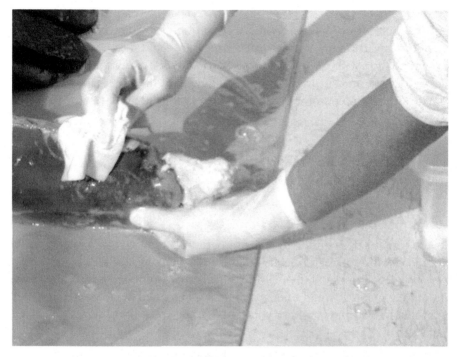

Winter's daily debriding and wound treatment

Dolphins require the use of their tail flukes to navigate through water, so we were concerned that without these, she could sink to the bottom of the small rehab pool and be unable to return to the surface. Since dolphins are mammals—thus air-breathing—they have to make a conscious decision to return to the surface to take a breath. While Winter might decide to swim to the surface, she may be unable to. That was only one of many challenges our sick and injured baby dolphin faced.

Our team rallied around this little fighter to give her every chance of living. Even though Winter had no credible long-term path of survival, we weren't about to give up. Instead, we continued to refuse calls to euthanize her. Because we didn't have a lot of answers, it all came down to this ...

Winter's will to fight would become the deciding factor in whether or not she would survive.

The Rise of Winter & Clearwater Marine Aquarium

I was kept up-to-date on Winter's condition every day. I dreaded any after-hours calls from my staff as I knew what they could mean. However, slowly at first and then with gathering momentum, Winter began to rally. She continued to improve and surprised us almost daily. The calls to euthanize her began to fade away. Winter simply tossed aside every hurdle life threw at her as if it was no big deal:

> *Severe infections? Who cares!*
>
> *Lost my tail flukes? So what!*
>
> *Learn to swim in a completely new way all by myself? I got this!*

You might say swimming upstream became a lifestyle for Winter, one she embraced with grace and determination. As the days and weeks passed, we were privileged to watch the real-life miracle that would soon inspire millions around the globe. I would often stand beside her small rehab pool and just be amazed at her attitude and her youthful fighting spirit. And her cuteness? Off the charts.

Winter eventually learned how to shimmy her way around the pool in a side-to-side motion and surface for air as needed. That was huge, as it became clear she could maneuver for breaths without assistance. It was also something she had learned to do on her own, so it was a major milestone indeed for this little fighter.

Then came the next blow. We noticed her spine becoming distorted by her newfound swimming pattern, and that was a problem. A big problem. What do we do now? This was another first. No one in the world had dealt with this, which caused us to doubt whether or not we were doing the right thing. Were we trying too hard to save one dolphin? Had we lost sight of reason living in our own little bubble?

Nevertheless, we forged ahead. Early on, we had discussed the idea of making a prosthetic tail as therapy for Winter's back. That would allow her to swim in a normal swimming pattern. Let's just say very few people took us seriously. "What? You've got to be nuts to try that!" Well, call me nuts if you want, but that's exactly what we did. It didn't happen overnight, though. First, I had to hit the marketing trail.

Considering all of Winter's needs, and with little money to operate and even less organizational vision in place when I took over, my job was to be the change agent if CMA were to survive. I had to be a disruptor. If I weren't, we would close. It was that simple and that stressful. Worse yet, only a few members of the team I inherited were up for the task.

There was no doubt that CMA's mission was great and noble, but it was underfunded and unorganized. So while I was overseeing the complex and complete total reorganization of CMA (fixing shaky roofs, getting up to speed with OSHA, USDA and other regulatory bodies, etc.), in the back of my mind, I knew I needed a story to tell. It had to be a BIG story to spread the word about our mission, and I needed it now.

My IRONMAN experience taught me how to spot a great story. Now, in Winter, I saw a truly phenomenal one unfolding right before my eyes. As I watched our team work with Winter and witnessed her struggle to survive, I instinctively knew I had been gifted what I needed to keep CMA alive, get our educational messages out and perhaps inspire others along the way.

Groundhog Day and a New Movement

IRONMAN was a catalyst for a movement centered on overcoming obstacles. Now, with respect to Winter's story, all I had to do was get the word out to the public to do the same.

That was no different than beginning a national advertising campaign for a new brand of health food. Since we had no funds whatsoever for any such campaign, I went big and used the best free advertising tool available: *the media*. Love 'em or hate 'em, they have reach. My IRONMAN days were about to help me launch another movement. At that point, CMA and Winter were virtually unknown. I was about to change that, positively disrupting millions of lives with our story.

I saw Winter's story as transcendently powerful, able to impact anyone and everyone, no matter what generation. An adorable and severely disabled baby dolphin who lost her tail and refused to give up and is now having a prosthetic tail developed. Dang! If you can't pitch that, it's time to pack it in and go home to mama.

If you're going to dream, make it a big one. I wanted Winter to have her own BIG LIFE, so my early goals for her story were a book, a documentary, and the big kahuna—a major motion picture. Why not? With that in mind, we launched what would become one of the most extensive animal-based media campaigns in history, designed to drive awareness of CMA's great mission.

What followed were hundreds of national news stories, including six *NBC Today Show* segments, five appearances on the *CBS Early Show*, time on *Good Morning America,* two appearances on *Oprah,* and hundreds of articles in magazines such as *National Geographic, Reader's Digest,* and *People,* to name a few. In fact, there weren't many magazines, newspapers, or news platforms across the world that did not carry Winter's story at least once. It was endless. It seemed the world couldn't get enough.

Business sign in Clearwater

I stumbled across an inspirational, once-in-a-lifetime story, and I wasn't afraid to tell it. When I released Winter's story, chapter by chapter, most media platforms ran it multiple times. Like the popular movie *The Truman Show* starring Jim Carrey, the world kept up with Winter's progress in real time.

While the media attention continued to grow, we focused on getting Winter her new tail, a project that was a mile outside everyone's box. Many thought we were in la-la land.

Then came the call.

Winter's peduncle

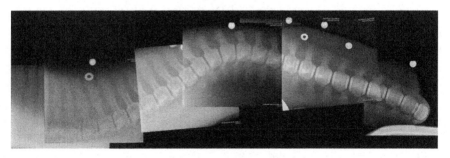

Winter's spine via multiple x-rays – 2011

"I always like to say that if David Yates wakes up in the morning and sees a mountain has been put in his path, that he takes one look at the mountain and says, 'No problem, I'll move it.'"

~ Austin Highsmith – Dolphin Tale actor

Perspiration Follows Inspiration

Tell your story ... and watch for good things to follow, right? A call came in from a man named Kevin Carroll, a renowned prosthetic engineer with an organization called Hanger Clinic. Kevin heard Winter's story on a national radio show segment and decided to contact us. He first contacted one of my team members. Then he and I talked. Or I should say he talked, and I listened. I was intrigued.

Kevin asked me about Winter's problem and her massive medical complications. It was a lot to absorb, but he never wavered. He felt Hanger Clinic could make a prosthetic tail for Winter and seemed personally challenged by the prospect. We ended the call with a commitment to follow up soon.

My team and I were not convinced, but I wanted to move on it, particularly after discovering more about the Hanger organization. It was founded by James E. Hanger, the first amputee in the American Civil War. Unwilling to spend the rest of his life unable to walk, Mr. Hanger invented a revolutionary prosthetic leg called the "Hanger Limb" for himself, then began manufacturing the devices to aid fellow wounded soldiers. Now that's a visionary.

Kevin called up one of his practitioner buddies, Dan Strzempka, and told him about the idea. Dan's response was, "Wait, you want me to do what?" Ha! But Dan was an amputee himself. Having lost a leg in a mowing accident at age four, he had personally experienced the benefits of prosthetics. After the call, he was all in. We were getting closer, but I knew if we had any chance of success with this project, I needed a strong team.

Early in 2007, I organized the Tail Development Team. Our members included Kevin and Dan from Hanger, two CMA dolphin team members, two of our marine mammal veterinarians, two members of a partner rescue organization, and me. The initial meetings (and there were many) included a lot of blue-skying followed by nuts-and-bolts discussions about the project's complications. I told my team to think of ourselves as akin to NASA—time to find a way to the moon!

Blue-sky /ˌbloo̅ˈskī/: *To make impractical or as yet unachievable plans*

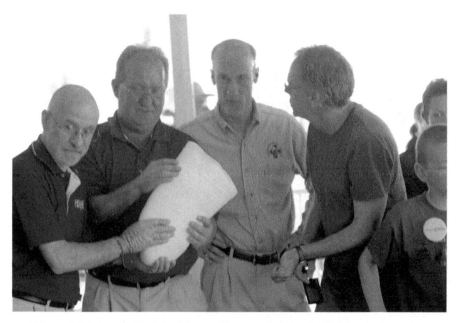

The real-life guys behind the Morgan Freeman role in the Dolphin Tale movies, Dan and Kevin on the left. Me in the middle. Casting Winter for a tail – 2010.

A Roller Coaster of a Week

While life at CMA rolled along, and we expanded our inspirational reach to kids worldwide, the Yates family was going to need some inspiration ourselves. It happened when one of our children had a medical emergency and nearly died. Having gone to an amusement park to ride the roller coasters, each time we tried to get on a different one, we were stopped. It was bizarre, and we knew something was up when FOUR roller coasters developed issues just when we got in line. A few days later, our child was found to have a heart issue that was unknown and undetected at the time. If we had gone on the coasters, who knows what would have happened? This was no coincidence but providence. God was looking after the Yates family. After extensive medical care the heart issue was resolved.

When we find ourselves helpless, let's look to someone other than ourselves. I am a Christian and a firm believer in the power of prayer. I believe God moves mountains every day.

The Tale of a Tail Begins

"Always listen to the experts.
They'll tell you what can't be done and why. Then do it."

~ Robert A. Heinlein

This book is about dreaming, throwing undue caution to the wind, and leaving the naysayers behind to lead a BIG LIFE. When we began making the famed Winter's Tail, many thought we were nuts. It was hard to argue with them. It sounded crazy. Why spend this much time and this many resources on one little dolphin? What if I had caved to the negativity? After all, I could have stopped the whole crazy project right then and there, and no one would have been the wiser. Tens of thousands of sick and injured kids would never have their life-changing inspiration, and nobody would ever have known. The *Dolphin Tale* franchise would never have seen the light of day, and CMA would remain the small, struggling facility it had been.

It would have been easy to forgo this crazy dream. Oh, but there's a fine line between crazies and world-changers; abandoning the project would have been a small life decision, not a big life decision. Sorry, but speaking for CMA and the Hanger Clinic teams—we chased *BIG DREAMS,* and we weren't afraid to swim upstream for them.

First Things First

Our earliest and most significant challenge was developing a prosthetic tail that would stay secure on Winter's body—with nothing to attach it to. Since dolphins have smooth and sensitive skin, it presented a serious dilemma: It had to be tight enough to stay on, yet not too tight to cause discomfort. If Winter didn't like the feel of the prosthetic, she would reject it, and the project would be over before it started. You can explain to a human how their prosthetic may be uncomfortable yet have a positive effect on their life, but you can't tell that to a dolphin. Our device had to be comfortable, and it had to fit. It was another mountain to climb, and the odds were not in our favor.

In our first movie, *Dolphin Tale,* you see the issue played out between Sawyer and Winter in a scene where Sawyer finally realizes why Winter isn't accepting the tail; the issue was the "sock," or, in medical terms, the "gel liner." To solve the matter, Dr. McCarthy (played by Morgan Freeman) comes up with the magic formula called "Winter's Gel." When he applies it, the tail works perfectly.

Note: Sorry for the crushing news, but no, Morgan Freeman didn't make the tail or the gel. I know that makes me a buzzkill, but in real life, the gel really is called "Winter's Gel," and Winter's tail really did work with the gel!

Scene from Dolphin Tale

As we moved ahead, ideas for the tail initially came from human prosthetic technology. But it wasn't easy. Like the gel, nearly everything about the tail had to be "MacGyvered" (check it out … a late-'80s TV series about an innovative crime-solving hero). For example, we knew that when it came time for Winter to try the tail for the first time, we had to have her fully prepared and desensitized. We couldn't just show up and say, "Here you go, Winter, put your tail on!" Ha!

Our team took small pieces of the gel to prepare her and placed them around her peduncle to get her used to the feel. Then, using their hands, they gently moved her body in up and down motions, mimicking a normal dolphin swimming pattern. Ever since she was three months old, Winter had been swimming in a side-to-side motion, and now she was nearly two years old. We were concerned she wouldn't be able to adjust back to a normal swimming motion. Who could tell?

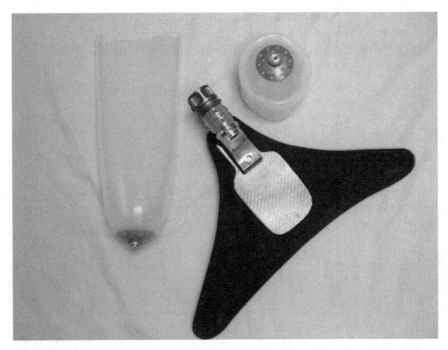

Early prosthetic tail parts – 2007

It was all a gamble. We were in uncharted waters (literally), and we knew we could spend months or even years developing a tremendous high-tech tail, only to have her reject it or not be able to adjust to it. The biggest problem was that Winter's spine and lateral muscles had adapted to her alternate swimming pattern, and we didn't know if this was permanent. Other challenges with the tail included weight, size, buoyancy, which materials to use, and "hot spots" on Winter's skin caused by friction. For the latter, we used thermography early on to scan Winter's peduncle and see where friction and heat were the greatest. Theoretically, once we knew, we could adjust the tail design accordingly. Most of the prosthetic tail is made from thermoplastic elastomer (science lesson for the day).

As our Tail Development Team continued to discuss the problems and thrash out solutions, Winter's international fame continued to grow. Finally, after passing the six-month mark, we had the first tail ready to go.

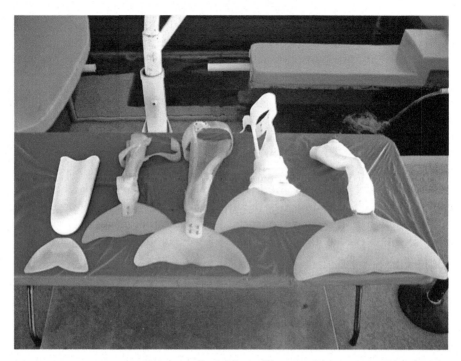

Various tail models used by Winter

A lot was on the line for Winter and CMA. First and foremost, if the tail didn't work, what would happen to Winter's spine? Would she be able to survive long term? Aside from that, what would happen to CMA and its reputation? Even before the movies came out, I had already built a global following for Winter, so this was a high-pressure moment with many waiting to see what would happen. Remember Geraldo Rivera and Al Capone's safe? Google it.

It was an overcast Monday morning in September of 2007 when our team gathered with guarded optimism. We had waited months to see if our hard work would pay off. Winter's skin had been desensitized with the hope that she would accept a foreign object on her peduncle. But would she? No one had ever done this before, so it felt a little like being the first to walk on the moon. Yet, it's in these types of pivotal moments that history is made.

Our team slid into the water on Winter's favorite platform and called Winter over as soon as everyone was in place. After a few moments of bonding, to make sure Winter was comfortable, Abby Stone (playing the proverbial role of Neil Armstrong), along with another caregiver, would be the first to put the tail on Winter. It was in Abby's hands, and we all watched, mesmerized, as she slowly brought the tail closer to Winter. When the prosthetic touched her body, Winter remained calm. It all came down to the relationship between this young dolphin and her caregivers. Not unlike a free-spirited wild stallion and his owner, Winter had, in time, accepted her caregivers as family. She trusted them, and most importantly, she trusted their touch.

Winter was calm but curious. As long as she accepted what we were doing, we could proceed. It took just a few moments while we held our breath. The silence was deafening, and you could cut the tension in the air with a dull knife. Remember those few minutes in the Apollo 13 flight when the crew was out of contact as they entered the earth's atmosphere? The world held its collective breath until their communication came back. That was a little like how I felt. Running through my mind were the months of hard work and effort put into this little dolphin who had become our family and this seemingly crazy idea, not to mention the fact that our reputations were on the line.

Then the tail was on!

At first she seemed to be okay with what was happening to her. I say that because she had quite a personality and would let you know very clearly if she was unhappy. She was a little unsure of what the new tail was and how to use it, but at least she did not reject it. The pre-planning had worked. We didn't want to be greedy, so we gently slipped the prosthetic tail off after a few minutes. Whew!

That was our initial attempt, and we all agreed that with that "first small step," the "eagle," er ... dolphin, may have landed (tired of the NASA clichés yet?). In any case, the Winter's Tail project was going swimmingly (see what I did there?), and we hoped Winter had a bright future. Sure, many adjustments would have to be made—some of which she would not be fond of—but at that moment, instinctively, we felt success was within our reach.

It wasn't only the tail that inspired the world. Winter's Gel also made a BIG splash.

"Dreaming permits each and every one of us to be quietly and safely insane every night of our lives."

~ William Dement

Winter's Gel Becomes a Hit

Inventors dream. Part of the excitement of developing Winter's Tail was attempting something nobody else had ever done. We were the Apollo 11 team, and we loved it. Many who heard about our project laughed at us and thought we were heading to Mars. But being "way out there" is where world-changers hang out. Einstein, Edison, Jobs, you name it; they were all a little crazy, but did their naysayers stop them? If you're holding an iPhone or using electricity, I guess not.

Every major advancement in society comes with a little eccentricity. Visionaries make waves and bring disruption while everyone else follows. That's what happened with Winter's Gel. Then we found out—quite by accident and from the mouth of a child—that it could help something other than dolphins: that would be humans. Kevin Carroll of Hanger explains:

"Before trying the gel on Winter, we put it on Dan Strzempka to make sure there wouldn't be any skin reactions. Typically, it is the other way around; those healthcare products are tested on animals first. But not for Winter. When news got out that Winter was using this special gel and having great success with it, a little girl from the West Coast who couldn't use her prosthetics asked us to try it on her. We did, and it was a major success. She continues to be successful with it to this day. Next came a young soldier who was nearly killed by a bomb in Iraq and badly injured. Prosthetic-wise, he wasn't doing very well, so I introduced him to Winter's Gel. In fact, I showed him how I could literally stand on my head with comfort to prove this was the stuff for him. It worked and allowed him to walk in comfort. Today, thousands of people are using Winter's Gel all over the world with great success, and as we all know, Winter continues to be an inspiration to us all."

Winter's Gel

Since the gel's invention, I have met hundreds of Hanger Clinic prosthetic patients who have quite confidently and proudly strolled into Clearwater Marine Aquarium wearing their Winter's Gel. They love the fact that they're using the same material used by the famous Winter. As for Hanger Clinic, the Winter's Tail project has been an enormous tool in convincing kids to wear their prosthetic legs or arms. We've met hundreds of their patients.

Winter was growing, the tail was working, the world was watching, and the little Superman boy from the beginning of the book was soaring. I found my wings despite my past, and I was living my purpose. Have you been moving towards fulfilling your dreams and finding your purpose? If not, now's the time! Check out my next dream. It's a doozy. But first, here's a dose of Winter's inspiration. That little dolphin just didn't quit!

Ellie's Story: Who Says I Can't Swim?

Ellie Challis should not be alive. She was just sixteen months old when she caught a deadly strain of meningitis, and the illness caused her heart to stop beating for two minutes. Even though the doctors said Ellie's chance of survival was a meager five percent, she fought through and made it. Sadly, deterioration from the disease forced the doctors to amputate much of her arms and her legs.

Ellie felt an immediate connection with Winter when she first watched *Dolphin Tale* and was amazed that it was based on a true story. Just like Ellie, Winter's chance of survival was very slim, and just like Ellie, Winter lost part of her body. Never ones to give up, Winter and Ellie surprised everyone by surviving, thriving, and excelling.

Ellie's dream came true in 2013 when she traveled from her home in England to Clearwater to meet Winter, her role model. That visit inspired Ellie so much that it motivated her to learn to swim despite her disability. Ellie says, "If Winter can swim without her tail, then I can swim without my arms and legs." And swim, she did. Ellie's persistence, incredible swimming skills and determination placed her on the English para swim team. She went on to win a medal at the Paralympics and holds a World Record! Wow. Go, Ellie, go!

7

WINTER ON THE BIG SCREEN: THE MAKING OF *DOLPHIN TALE*

A Movie? You're Crazy, Yates!

Nobody believed I could pull off a major motion picture. Nobody. Not even my cat. Maybe my dog, but definitely not my cat. Even people in my organization thought I was nuts. But what others believed didn't matter to me: it was what I believed that mattered. That said, I couldn't blame them. What were the odds that a former accountant and a disabled dolphin could team up to save CMA and, in the process, reach the world?

Telling Winter's story

As I mentioned before, I launched the Winter the Dolphin media campaign in September of 2006 to drive CMA awareness and increase our financial support through increased attendance and donations. For CMA, the timing was perfect and kicked off a massive, four-year global media binge of Winter's ongoing story. The world could not get enough of this baby dolphin survivor. That put me on the path to both *Dolphin Tale* movies and more.

Telling Winter's story again

In early 2007, I received a call from Dave Fierson, head of the legal department at Alcon Entertainment, an independent Hollywood film company that distributed its movies via Warner Bros. Not knowing who I was, he introduced himself and said they were interested in making a movie about Winter. After almost dropping the phone, I composed myself. The concept he put forward was to have Winter help save people during Hurricane Katrina or something imaginative like that. I had just been in general conversations with a group in New York about the possibility of a movie based on Winter's story. The vision was just beginning to unfold, so this call from Alcon ramped up the movie conversations on all fronts.

During our conversation, I told him who I was and about my background with IRONMAN. He seemed surprised and mentioned that one of Alcon's Co-CEOs, Andrew Kosove, is a long-term IRONMAN athlete himself who loves the IRONMAN fitness lifestyle. As it turns out, Andrew Kosove also happens to be a highly successful Hollywood executive, along with his partner Broderick Johnson, with movies like *My Dog Skip, Prisoners,* and the Oscar-nominated *The Blind Side* under their belts. They were shocked to know I was the guy running CMA. They were just cold calling the "CEO at CMA," whoever that may be. It felt like that Disneyland ride: It's a small, small world.

Dave and I spent hours on the phone over the next several months discussing the project. Looking back, I felt the same excitement and hopefulness I did when I negotiated the IRONMAN purchase. Groundhog Day again. Both were huge deals that would impact the world if successful. The Alcon relationship felt right from the start, so off we went. Over time we all became great friends and remain so to this day.

In Development

We gave Alcon back-to-back options on the film, which meant they had the right to vet the story before committing to producing the film. In the movie industry, it's called getting the "greenlight," and very few scripts make it that far. To keep my end of the deal, I kept pumping the media with Winter's story to build pre-awareness and momentum for the potential movie. I had worked on the TV side of things during my IRONMAN years, and now I was about to dive deep into the world of filmmaking.

Alcon became convinced of the movie's potential, so they developed the script with my good friends Richard Ingber, Alcon's head of marketing, and writer/producer Noam Dromi, who teamed to initially bring the project to the company. As the development process unfolded, Alcon brought in veteran screenwriter Karen Janszen, whose credits included *Free Willy 2,* to work on the screenplay, so it was a logical fit from a film genre perspective.

The script eventually went to well-known actor/writer/director Charles Martin Smith, and once he made his changes, it was off to the races. Soon thereafter, Alcon announced their intentions to the media ... on my birthday, nonetheless. Best gift in years ...

Los Angeles, California; December 8, 2009:

Warner Bros.-based Alcon Entertainment will finance and produce the feature "Dolphin Tale" for Charles Martin Smith ("Air Bud") to write and direct. It was announced by Alcon co-founders and co-CEOs Andrew Kosove and Broderick Johnson. Richard Ingber of Alcon Entertainment will also produce.

The film will be released through Alcon's output deal with Warner Bros. Inspired by the true story of "Winter" the dolphin, "Dolphin

Tale" is about a young boy who befriends an injured dolphin who lost her tail in a crab trap. Through their bond and friendship, the boy motivates everyone around him to help save the dolphin by creating a prosthetic appendage to replace the dolphin's missing tail. Winter's strong survival instincts become an inspiration to people with special needs throughout the world.

Alcon Entertainment's Steve Wegner developed the take that Smith will write. David Fierson secured the rights from Clearwater Marine Aquarium and David Yates. Smith, who is also a successful actor with credits including "Never Cry Wolf" and "The Untouchables," recently wrote and directed "Stone of Destiny," starring Charlie Cox, Kate Mara, and Robert Carlyle for Arclight Films.

My purpose was expanding, and I knew it. I wanted a BIG LIFE. That little boy in the Superman suit who was separated from his schizophrenic mom; that teen who had battled it out with his stepmom and got into mountains of trouble; the guy who was unceremoniously fired from his first real job, and who everyone thought would never be a success, was ready to fly. I was learning the discipline of swimming upstream, and I saw the fruits of it.

Fulfilling a big purpose takes tenacity, but I was getting closer. That was the first press release announcing *Dolphin Tale* as a bona fide major motion picture. A greenlight was ever nearer, and the project went from slow motion to rocket speed overnight. Now the real task began with picking the right actors from a pool of the best talent.

Meanwhile, the project ran into a "minor" hurdle called "film incentives." Producers are typically presented with incentives by different states to attract film and TV projects. Effectively, these corporate incentives are used to convince a studio to film in their state rather than another. They can also play a role in determining whether or not a movie is greenlit at all.

Like any product or service vying for market share, the bar is set once any state antes up incentives. Among my tasks at CMA was to dig into the incentives issue for ways our area could be more competitive. Amazingly, I found that incentives were offered in many states but not Florida at that time. And what happens when incentives don't exist in a state? A good example is the Ben Affleck movie *Live by Night,* a gangster flick set partially in the area of Tampa called Ybor City. You would assume they filmed it in the actual Ybor City, right? That would be wrong. Due to Georgia's state incentives, the studio actually saved money by erecting a fake Ybor City in Brunswick, Georgia. I'm not kidding. Why build a set in another state instead of shooting the film in the actual Ybor City? Georgia offered incentives at the time, and Florida did not. Sad but true.

While the incentive issue was being worked on, we went full steam ahead with what is called "pre-production." Everything picked up speed, particularly the vital cast selection process, which was quite interesting to watch. If the wrong person is cast in a role, it can seriously damage a movie or TV show. Imagine casting Pee Wee Herman instead of Harrison Ford for the role of US president in the film *Air Force One*. Okay, that's a bit extreme, but you get my point.

Making movies is costly, and they have financial risk, so all the pieces have to fit together. The elements of writing, cast selection, choosing the director, and funding for starters all have to synergize if the production is going to "pop." As one of my studio partners put it, "I go to Vegas to get away from gambling!" The point is that every Hollywood project is a gamble, and we only know if the risk pays off on the day the movie opens to the public. Though we may work for three or four years on a film, we have to wait 'til the day of release to find out if it was all worth it. It's a crazy but exciting business, and it was a bit scary for us at this point because we still lacked film incentives. Without incentives from the State of Florida, my three-year dream and all my hard work would likely go down the drain, and the naysayers would be right.

Greenlight

Thankfully, and literally in the nick of time, the Florida legislature passed a budget in May 2010 that included new film incentives. God winked at us once again. Whew! When the governor signed it into law, we were off to the races. The greenlight quickly followed.

Don't believe the naysayers and dream killers. Don't just look for a dream for your life; look for the Pipe Dream, the BIG dream God put in your heart that you know you can achieve. Then have a plan, and you're off to the races. That's what I did.

The phrase "Pipe Dream" reportedly originated in an 1890 issue of the *Chicago Daily Tribune,* referring to the crazy and unachievable idea of aerial navigation. How'd that work out? Not too shabby. Pipe dreams are a good thing.

The A-List

There were several big roles to cast, and watching the process was surreal. First up was the CMA's executive director role. The original screenwriter spent some time talking with me and said she based the role on my persona, but in the end, it was more of a fictionalized person.

Alcon approached Harry Connick, Jr., who had been in a previous Alcon movie, *P.S. I Love You*. After he went through our script, Harry loved the idea and took the role.

From there, we needed to cast the prosthetist's role. For the sake of the movie, this role became an amalgamation of our two Hanger Clinic partners. Everyone initially had their eye on Robin Williams for the role since he had starred in a previous Alcon film, *Insomnia*. Most of us involved in the film assumed Robin would be cast, but he had a scheduling conflict and declined the offer. That was a shame because, in everyone's estimation, Robin would have been perfect for that quirky role, sort of like Mork meets Winter the dolphin. Think about that one for a while.

As it goes with popular actors, scheduling conflicts are often the reason for unavailability. If they can't make it when you need them, that's that, and you move on to the next choice. That said, Alcon decided to take a shot at none other than a little-known actor named Morgan Freeman. You may have heard of him. Morgan had never been in an Alcon film, but he would be perfect for the role with his great comedic side.

Once selected as a candidate, we all wondered if he would accept the role. At that point in his career, he could have done anything he wanted, and he seemed to be in nearly every top film that came along. To our pleasant surprise, he was all in. By landing Morgan, we'd basically "defaulted" to an Academy Award-winning actor. Ha!

The other A-list roles were filled by Ashley Judd (Lorraine Nelson, the mom) and the legendary Kris Kristofferson (Reed Haskett, the old sage). However, filling the roles of the two kids, Sawyer and Hazel, was a bit trickier. As important as it was to have big names in the film—and we did—we knew if those two roles didn't connect with the audience, the film would suffer.

After a lengthy casting process, Cozi Zuehlsdorff was selected for the role of Hazel Haskett. Cozi, who was 12 years old at the time, would soon gain success on multiple Disney TV shows. She was a perfect fit for the role. Next up was the vital role of Sawyer, the shy kid who connected to Winter. Ultimately, that role went to Nathan Gamble. Nathan was also twelve at the time, and by then, he already had an impressive portfolio with credits such as *Batman: The*

Dark Knight, playing Brad Pitt's son in *Babel,* and a hit family film, *Marley and Me.* Nathan had won the role, but he needed one more endorsement before he was cast. The final vote would have to come from the eminent star of the movie. Winter, of course. Once they spent some time together, she raised her fin in approval.

Once that hurdle was over, the remaining positions were filled. Sawyer's cousin, the role-model-turned-wounded-vet, was played by Austin Stowell (*Whiplash, Bridge of Spies, Battle of the Sexes*), while Austin Highsmith (*Scream, CSI, Rogues of LA*) was selected for the role of the dolphin trainer. Now that we had our A-listers along with a few up-and-coming stars, we began prepping for a fall 2010 shooting schedule.

Initiating Warp Speed

If I thought I was busy before, what came next tripled our workload. A staggering amount of things had to be done and done on time—because time was money. Now with the assurance of state incentives, with actors lined up and a myriad of other details set in motion, we no longer had the option of changing the schedule. What made things even tighter was the fact that the animals had to be ready for their roles too.

Who says movie production isn't high-tech?
A gas can and duct tape in action, getting Winter used to what was to come.

Our CMA staff went from zero to one hundred mph learning all the duties involved with filmmaking. None of them had ever been involved in filmmaking. Most importantly, we all agreed we would not, and could not, stop our core work of marine life rescue, which is the backbone for our educational mission.

Because Winter didn't know a thing about schedules, it was up to us to be sure she was well-prepped for what she would see and do. Everyone agreed we would only do what Winter wanted to do. To that point, during the writing process, I mentioned to the director that he should spend time at CMA to observe what Winter does on a daily basis because she does some hilariously cute things on her own. The idea was for him to observe the things Winter already does and write them into the script, rather than writing things we wanted her to do. In short, as much as possible, we wanted to let Winter be Winter.

The perfect example of this is a hilarious scene in the first movie where Winter, Hazel and Sawyer are relaxing on floating mats in the pool. Using a little Hollywood magic, we filmed that scene with three people in the water holding the mats so they would stay together. Later they were edited out. Winter was never the wiser as to how we did it. She was just having fun. She did that in real life without cameras, and it always cracked us up.

Here is the movie version:

And here is real life:

Some wonder how we filmed Winter in so many scenes, including scenes outside our facility. Well, there were actually three Winter's in the movies. Every actor has a stand-in double, right? First, there was Winter herself. Most scenes that were inside our facility were the real Winter. Second, we used CGI in some scenes shot outside our facility, such as the "Save Winter Day" scene in the first movie. Finally, for the Winter rescue scene filmed at Honeymoon Island in the neighboring city of Dunedin, a robotic-type Winter was made (technically called an animatronic) by the well-known special makeup effects artist Howard Berger and his team (*The Walking Dead, The Amazing Spider-Man 2, Lone Survivor*). No one was the wiser as they did a great job making Winter the animatronic look like Winter the marine mammal. Off-screen, the team operated the James Bond version of Winter. So much for telling my kids you can't make a living playing video games! The bottom line was we filmed Winter in her natural role and then used other creative methods.

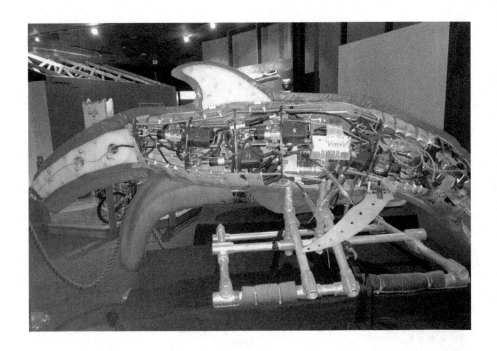

From the time she was young, Winter's personality seemed to be, "Who cares if I lost my tail? You're the different one, not me!" She was incredibly cute and playful. Not until she got a little older did she become a little more serious. That was especially true when she was around the ridiculously playful young dolphin, Hope, whom you will meet later.

Showtime: A Dream Fulfilled

When the actors and crew arrived and filming started, reality began to set in, especially for our team. Dang. It was really happening. But if my team expected a fast-paced production, they were in for a surprise. Things don't move so quickly on a movie set. In fact, they move slowly. Very slowly. Each scene was shot multiple times. Every shadow was considered, and expressions have to be just what the director wants to carry the story forward.

As the cast continued to arrive, CMA became a magical place. I could be sitting at my desk, and all of a sudden, Morgan Freeman or Harry Connick, Jr. might stroll by. The first time Harry arrived, I took him on a tour of CMA. I'm not typically starstruck, but this was Harry Connick, Jr., after all. I quickly found out that everything you hear about Harry being a great guy is absolutely true. It's real. We also discovered he has a great sense of humor; I mean Robin Williams kind of funny. Often when Harry was on the set, he caused the other actors to crack up while the cameras were rolling. I remember listening to the filming audio on our headsets, and Harry's comments between takes made us roll out of our chairs with laughter.

Another surprise was Morgan Freeman, who occasionally broke into song on the set. We thought it was ironic because Harry was the legendary singer, yet Morgan was the one who sang on the set. And he has a pretty good voice too. I enjoyed talking to him; at a VIP beach party, Morgan grabbed my wife, Joan, and reminded me I was lucky he didn't find her first. He's right.

Much of my work on the set was to problem-solve with Bob Engelman, the line producer. Bob and I spent many hours in the trenches figuring out how to film a major motion picture in a marine life rescue center with ongoing operations. When it was time to feed our sea turtles, guess what? That's what we did, and filming would have to wait. We also took over the entire neighborhood, including the nearby Catholic church, where we put our foodservice and the costume design departments. Thank you, Vatican! Each evening we would watch what is called "dailies." These are clips of what was filmed that day to see if we captured what we needed. Filming is an around-the-clock adventure. All the local politicians, community leaders, CEOs, and everyone else who considered themselves essential showed up on the set. Some of my time was spent giving private tours to these VIPs. Everyone who was anyone locally wanted a chance to be on the set.

Out of My Hands

After three months of filming, it was time to wrap. Next came post-production, marketing, the eventual Hollywood and local premieres, and finally, the theatrical release. In the run-up to the release, dealing with media, screenings and premieres was an experience I'll never forget. Surreal. The local excitement was at a crescendo with growing community awareness. Little old Clearwater was about to be featured in a worldwide major motion picture by Alcon Entertainment and Warner Bros. It's hard to express the excitement and sense of accomplishment I felt knowing the world was about to experience a movie about something I had both lived through and produced. The buzz started in the spring and kept building until the crescendo at the Hollywood premiere in September. I did interview after interview as our local area began to be lit about what was coming. CMA was the talk of the state.

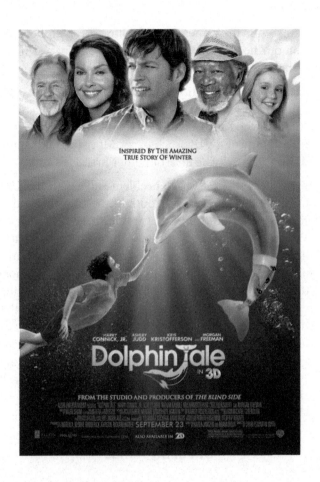

After the LA premiere, we staged a premiere of *Dolphin Tale* in Clearwater at Ruth Eckerd Hall, a famous concert facility. I brought in a 3-D theatrical system from Los Angeles, and we built a theater inside the concert hall. We hired the same production team that did the outdoor 3-D premiere of *Avatar*. Hey, I wasn't about to be outdone by James Cameron! The only problem was that the electricity went out 20 minutes into the premiere. Not kidding. Thankfully, our state utility provider president was in the house and resolved the problem pronto. When the movie was released, I often went to the theaters to see the crowds and see how the audiences reacted. It's not every day you get to do that.

As you move toward your BIG LIFE, find partners who can help you get to your destination. Going solo keeps you "so low."

I had many partners who contributed to my success. None more so than Alcon Entertainment, Governor Scott and the State of Florida, the City of Clearwater, Pinellas County, my CMA team including Frank Chivas, and Lew Friedland and the IRONMAN owners and team. Don't forget those that brought you to the dance.

Two weeks after *Dolphin Tale*'s premiere, it rose to be the #1 movie in North America, overtaking *The Lion King*'s re-release and *Moneyball* starring Brad Pitt. Not bad for a story about a disabled dolphin and a converted sewage treatment plant. The four years against-all-odds dream had landed. The Tampa area was over the top about the movie.

'DOLPHIN TALE' SLAYS 'LION KING' AT

BOX OFFICE

ENTERTAINMENT

'Dolphin Tale' dethrones 'The Lion King' with $14.2M for top movie

8

THE GREAT WORK OF CLEARWATER MARINE AQUARIUM

My BIG Purpose Becomes Clearwater's BIG Purpose

With the North American release of *Dolphin Tale* on September 23, 2011, and the global release in 42 countries soon thereafter, the world quickly took an interest in Clearwater Marine Aquarium. The result was millions of moviegoers making a pilgrimage to Clearwater to see the dolphin star of the movies, meet the real-life team featured in the films, explore our facilities, and hit the famous white sand of Clearwater Beach. People love to see the WOW factor of what they saw in a movie. It's akin to the millions who have traveled to the farm in rural Iowa where they filmed much of the Kevin Costner classic *Field of Dreams*. The difference is that while my little ol' Iowa isn't exactly the tourism capital of the world, Clearwater Marine Aquarium is situated in a prime Florida beach location only two hours from Disney World. People came in droves, the crowds surged, and they kept coming and coming. Our annual attendance skyrocketed from just over 76,000 in 2006 to around 740,000 the year after the movie release! People lined up around the block and completely overran our small facility. It was the talk of the state and even caught the attention of Florida's then-Governor Rick Scott, who visited CMA numerous times.

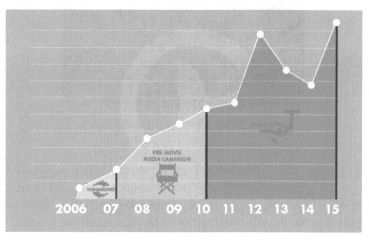

I had a vision. Nobody would stop it, and I had great partners and a great team to be sure it materialized. It was happening right before our eyes. Still, I knew my purpose was just becoming evident. I wasn't done reaching the world with a message, and neither was Winter. Our success led to a much greater ability to accomplish our core nonprofit mission of education, marine life rescue, and human inspirational connections. We began to build the needed infrastructure for our animal care work, more room for our guests, and we went from a staff of 35 to nearly 300! On any given day, you can find our team rescuing a sea turtle an hour away from our facility or partnering on the release of a rehabilitated manatee. We merged with a marine life research group that took our work to Belize, Cuba and beyond. You can find these team members flying up and down the East Coast, searching for an endangered whale species known as Right whales.

Whale photo survey team

We began to make substantial improvements to our aging facility and equipment to the point that we went from an industry laggard to an industry leader, and we were able to hire more experienced staff. The bottom line was our animal hospital became exactly that: a legitimate animal hospital with all the resources needed to fulfill that part of our mission. With our $80 million expansion ready to open, we went from this in 1980 ...

... to this in 2020

This progress was not always smooth sailing. There were many headwinds and much swimming upstream, even from some of those around me. Often, the sanity of my vision was questioned, but once it began to bear fruit, the naysayers typically fled for a while. What kept me on course when challenged? Belief in God's guidance, CMA's mission, and Winter's powerful story. I wasn't going to listen to the naysayers and dream killers, and neither should you.

Any successful person will tell you that opposition will often come from those closest to you, especially those who are envious of your success. What does a true leader do in that case? You keep moving and don't look back. Leaders lead; they don't follow.

Here are only a few examples of the inspiring marine life rescue work at CMA. Amazing people.

Sea Turtle Release Day – Going Home!

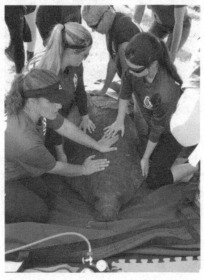

Hands-On Manatee Rescue – February 2017

Spinner Dolphin Rescue – 2017

Vision

The word "vision" is powerful when applied to the right purpose. Most dictionaries define the term as "the ability to think about or plan the future with imagination or wisdom." But there's a broader concept in the book of Proverbs: "Where there is no vision, the people perish." Perish? Really? That's a strong statement. Humans were built to look ahead in life, to envision greater things, and if there is nothing to look up to, their hope will fail. When hope fails, the spirit fails. God wired us to need vision. Think about it: What is life without the ability to dream? Dreaming is the fuel in the engine that drives our lives.

Every child has dreamed of being something, whether it is an NBA star (that would be me), an astronaut, a police officer, a Broadway star, or whatever. What is your dream?

Of course, not everything we dream comes true, but that's not the point. The ability to dream motivates our lives toward a BIG purpose; the flip side being, BIG purposes don't happen without a dream. Here are two individuals who took on some pretty rough waters in their upstream swim to fulfill their dreams:

Grace's Story: My Great-Uncle Did What?

Nine-year-old Grace Savage has DiGeorge syndrome, a chromosomal disorder resulting in poor development of several body systems. But Grace is a fighter, and she found a kindred spirit in Winter. With major surgeries being a "normal" thing for Grace, she needed a role model, somebody who had taken the journey she was on and had found their way through it. That "somebody" was Winter. When Grace discovered the *Dolphin Tale* movies, everything seemed to click. If this little dolphin named Winter could see past her struggles and thrive, so could Grace.

One day Grace was reading our Scholastic book about Winter when, lo and behold, she saw the fisherman's name that saved Winter and realized it was her own *Great-Uncle Jim Savage*! What? She had seen the real-life fisherman who rescued Winter depicted in *Dolphin Tale,* but incredibly, never knew it was actually a member of her own family. Jim Savage is a humble man and kept quiet about what he did. He enjoyed seeing his little rescued dolphin inspire tens of thousands of sick or special needs children, but Jim had no idea a member of his own family was one of them. After learning this, Grace and her family traveled to meet Jim at CMA for an inspiring and emotional family reunion. The moral of the story—pay it forward and watch it circle back to your life. Jim saved Winter, and Winter in turn helped save Grace. That's the way our world should work.

With Grace and Jim Savage – 2019

Levi's Story: A Life Connection

"I appreciate David so much for giving me the opportunity to be able to volunteer and now work as an employee at CMA. I hope that as I meet others with Autism, as well as other disabilities, that I can encourage and inspire them as David has with me."

~ Levi Larochelle

Levi Larochelle lives with Asperger's syndrome—an autism spectrum disorder. Life "on the spectrum" can be hard, and Levi had been spiraling downward as his condition worsened. He spent much of his time alone in his room, often curled up on the floor in a fetal position. Levi was fearful of a trip to the store and had no friends. Struggling to find some kind of solution for her son, his mom, Kim, contacted us to see if Levi could visit CMA, although she doubted Levi would actually take the step and do something away from home.

Children like Levi who live with autism do not do well with change. But after some motherly coaxing, Levi agreed to come see us, and to Kim's surprise he loved it! Having seen Winter in person and being enthralled with her story, Kim and I came up with an idea: Why not include Winter in Levi's therapeutic regimen, since being near her lit him up like never before? We thought it might enhance the effectiveness of his therapy. So that's what we did. On June 26, 2010, at the age of nine, Levi participated in the first of several of his therapeutic sessions with Winter.

Kim described the experience:

"I was dreading the encounter and couldn't sleep the night before because I knew Levi struggled with doing new things. But he went, so there we were, about to be with Winter for the very first time. Winter was a sweet little dolphin with a disability of her own, and Levi's face lit up when he saw her for the first time. His eyes danced with delight when he looked straight at her. Most amazing was the smile that spread across his face as if he had just seen his best friend. I was stunned because Levi had made his first social connection."

Levi's first connection with Winter

During the filming of both *Dolphin Tale* movies, I was able to get hundreds of people from our local community cast as extras, and Levi was one of them. The role of Sawyer, the shy, young lead character, had many similarities to Levi, but he was not aware of this as he had not seen the script. When we were filming the closing scene, the one where the uncomfortable and awkward Sawyer speaks to the crowd of people, Levi and Kim happened to be extras that day. During the filming, Levi started crying between takes. When Kim asked him why, he said, "Sawyer is just like me. He's me."

Sawyer's dock scene speech in Dolphin Tale

So let's recap. A real-life Sawyer connects with Sawyer's role while on the set as an extra filming an actual scene with Sawyer? That's amazing.

Today Levi is a happy, well-adjusted 21-year-old. Looking back to when I first met him, he couldn't look me in the eye. What a transformation, and just like Sawyer in the movie, I hired him. Levi now works at CMA. You can see a video on his story and others on my website at *DavidYatesInspire.com*. He and I attended an event last year where we both spoke, and he turned to me and said, "Mr. David, thank you for giving me a life."

I'm not crying; you're crying.

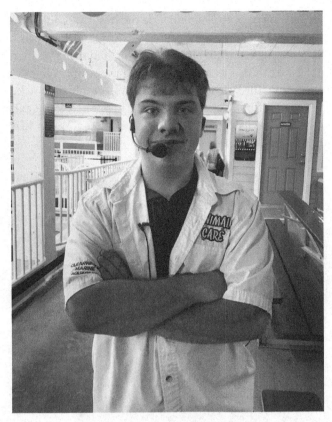

Levi – a real-life Sawyer

Making Hollywood History

I don't believe in fate. I believe in *providence*. As if one major motion picture wasn't enough, it was time to set a Hollywood record. Why not? Up to that point, there had never been a sequel to a movie based on real life. How would we do it? The second movie would have to come from additional real-life events, compelling enough to warrant greenlight status all over again. Sounds impossible, right? Wrong.

When your dream is on a roll, roll with it!

The closest movie to us in genre was *Free Willy*. That movie had two sequels. If your kids grew up in the '90s, you know about the *Free Willy* killer whale series. Well, one of our *Dolphin Tale* writers happened to write *Free Willy 2*, so why not dream about a sequel? The problem was the *Free Willy* series was fiction, while *Dolphin Tale* was based on real-life incidents.

Everyone in the know said a sequel to *Dolphin Tale* was not happening because there couldn't possibly be a second compelling real-life story to support it. An event like World War II can be told many times, in many ways, because of its complexity and fascination. But *Dolphin Tale* was a real one-time event about one dolphin: a one-in-a-million, no-holds-barred, complete story with nothing held back. There were no leftovers. At least that's what most people thought. Turns out, in the space of a few short hours, all that was about to change, and we would suddenly find ourselves on the journey to making Hollywood history.

Here's how it played out:

A Night to Remember

The last day of filming for *Dolphin Tale* was Saturday, December 11, 2010. After more than three years of hard work, we were ready to cross the finish line for filming and move on to post-production. As was typical with any movie, we planned a going away party known as a "wrap party," and it would take place at the renowned Island Way Grill restaurant next door to CMA, owned by CMA key board member Frank Chivas.

Around four in the afternoon, I went home to change clothes for the party. At five, I got a call from Bob Engelman, our line producer. Bob and I spent many days in the bunker solving production problems on the movie, and he called to say they had finished the last shot; we had wrapped! We let out a yippee or two and said we would meet at the party. That's when it got crazy, and movie history was set in motion.

Ten minutes after hanging up with Bob, I got another call. It was from a team member informing me that a baby dolphin had been rescued on Florida's east coast and would soon be en route to CMA for emergency care. Sound familiar? In this case, the dolphin was rescued while trying to nurse from its deceased mother. It was a sad situation, and we all assumed the dolphin would likely expire during the four-hour trip to CMA. Still, we prepared to intake the dolphin with the necessary medical equipment and supplies. We even brought in a crane to lift it to a second-story medical pool. It would be a few hours until they arrived, so my wife and I went next door to the party.

Eventually, the hustle and bustle concerning the rescue spread throughout the party. What was happening at CMA? Finally, around 11 p.m., as the party was winding down, the stranding van pulled up with the baby dolphin. We weren't sure what to expect. *Was it alive?*

What happened next would be depicted in *Dolphin Tale* 2, launching the first real-life sequel in Hollywood history.

9

A SECOND MIRACLE: THE MAKING OF
DOLPHIN TALE 2

Surreal Similarities

After the van carrying the rescued dolphin calf had backed into position, the rescue leader in charge of the transport, Steve McCulloch, quickly made his on-site assessment of staff and resources. After briefing the team, they slowly opened the door, allowing the dolphin calf to gradually adjust to the changes in temperature, light and sounds. The dolphin was still alive, but according to the attending veterinarian, Juli Goldstein, she was showing signs of distress and was just barely hanging on. Rather than waste precious time lifting her with the crane to the second-level pool, Steve gathered her in his experienced arms and carefully made his way up the stairs. On the way, Steve told me in hushed words that she was arching and holding her breath, signs a dolphin can be on the verge of dying. He knew what he was talking about as Steve is a legend in our industry, a one-of-a-kind Crocodile Hunter kind of guy I greatly respect.

Meanwhile, we had reduced our pool water level so our team could walk on the bottom while feeding and caring for her. This kind of rescue is always an intense hands-on process, and the initial transition and acclimation into a new environment often determine its success.

Steve carrying Hope
113

At the top of the stairs, the team was ready with a stretcher to carefully lower the critical dolphin into the pool. As soon as she entered the water she began struggling furiously, trying to break free to speed swim (which she eventually did). That might sound cute, but we knew that her speed swimming could be a precursor to complete exhaustion. In this situation (purely out of stress), she could literally swim herself to death. We got her slowed down and after she settled into the caring hands of our team, a long night of intensive care began. Eerily similar to when Winter came to us, I didn't know if she would survive until the morning. We knew how these things went, and it wasn't looking good.

Meanwhile, as the rescue was playing out at CMA, word began to spread throughout the party that something was transpiring. Several of the cast and crew ventured over to CMA to see what it was. Picture this: these actors and crew members had just completed filming a movie about Winter's rescue—now they got to watch a real-life rescue intake within minutes of wrapping the movie. *On the same night, during the wrap party!* Our last baby dolphin intake had been five years earlier. The timing was surreal, and the small crowd gathered there was abuzz. How could this happen? What were the odds? Some thought it was a prank on the crew, and some joked that we were filming a night scene for the movie.

After things settled down, I stood by the rail to watch our team work their magic. As I watched, I began to realize that what was unfolding before our eyes was crazier than anyone thought. The similarities between this dolphin and Winter were not just uncanny, but wildly so:

- Both dolphins are the same species - Atlantic bottlenose dolphins
- Both are female
- Both were 2–3 months old when rescued
- Both were rescued in the same area of Florida, just a few miles apart
- A rescuer named Teresa was involved in both rescues and held both Winter and this dolphin during the rescue
- This dolphin arrived five years and one day from the day Winter arrived

It's crazy that this happened to play out within minutes of filming the last scene of *Dolphin Tale*. I'm talking about minutes. God winked at us again.

What did I name this second little miracle dolphin? Hope. Why? Winter brought hope to millions, and I thought this little gal could too. I was about to be proven right.

Winter & Hope; Fast Friends – 2011

Déjà Vu

I admit it. As I watched Hope's arrival, I couldn't help but think, *Have I just been handed a story for a sequel?* I remembered how many people thought I was crazy chasing the first movie, but if I tell them about this idea, I would be certified insane! But I knew this could provide credible real-life content for a second movie, so I would have to let it play out for a while and keep my thoughts to myself. I also knew that to get the massive film production to CMA for a second time, I would need to be a force of nature again. I would have to lead the effort.

Putting the Pieces Together ... Again

I began with the basics. What's the first thing you need to pitch a movie? A story. So I took it upon myself to develop a "treatment"—a short summary of the sequel story. It would center on the events of the night Hope arrived and her resulting relationship with Winter. But I needed to build an entire story beyond just a simple rescue. So I went to work.

For the next six months, while Hope recuperated, I continued to write and edit until I thought there was a solid treatment for a second movie, one with enough sizzle and real-life elements to be credible and attention-getting. I reviewed previous compelling real-life incidents and moments at CMA from the last twenty years. Finally, I was done. To be certain everyone knew the story was anchored in real life, I highlighted the factual parts of the manuscript with yellow. I knew I needed more than one real-life element to get attention for the treatment, so I included several other compelling occurrences we experienced at CMA, ones we had not written into the first movie. Of course, Hope and Winter's new relationship was the core part of the story, but I added the real-life rescue, rehab, and release of a dolphin named Mandy, who was released with another dolphin named Troy in 2006.

Mandy release, Dunedin, FL Causeway, October 2006

Another key element I put into the treatment was the death of one of our beloved rescued dolphins named Panama. Panama was our oldest dolphin, and I knew that when she passed we would have a dilemma because she was Winter's social partner. What would Winter do without her partner? CMA doesn't buy, sell or breed dolphins, so we relied on rescued animals to establish the social networks they need. This potential dilemma provided an idea for the required tension needed in our second script. So I wrote in the treatment that Panama died, even though she was still alive at that time. In real life, Hope arrived before Panama died, but until Hope came on the scene, it was a real concern, and we played that out in the story. Little did I know that this aspect of the movie would play out just before filming. Sadly, while preparations for *Dolphin Tale* 2 were underway, less than two months before filming, Panama died, leaving Winter, her caregivers and all of us at CMA with a hole in our hearts. The movie became real life before it was even filmed. We filmed it in honor of Panama.

Winter & Panama

I can't count the number of times I pored over that treatment, but it was in the hundreds. Only when I felt I had the best story possible did I send it out to my partners with hope upon "Hope" that they would like it. Mind you, this was only the first step, but if I didn't clear this hurdle, it would be game over.

Then came the email that started the ball rolling.

"*David,*

There are some interesting thoughts in your document. Let us review internally this week, and then we can discuss further with you."

With that brief but telling email from Alcon, the development process for a Hollywood milestone had begun. Once more, we were off to the races, this time with *Dolphin Tale 2*. It would have the same cast, much of the same crew, many of the same extras and filmed mainly at CMA again. Charles Martin Smith wrote the full script. Groundhog Day. Again. All we needed was Bill Murray (it's a movie, friends, Google it).

Getting A-listers like Harry Connick, Jr., Morgan Freeman, Ashley Judd, and Kris Kristofferson to show up again at the same time, considering their crazy schedules, was a monumental challenge. If any of them were unavailable when we needed them, we would have a significant problem. Would they all come back? I'll get to that shortly.

"Ain't nothing better, we beat the odds together ..."

~ Shania Twain

A $10 Million Bet – Not Done Dreaming

Sing it, Shania. Once again, I was swimming upstream to a new purpose, and the burden was on my shoulders. To lock in a greenlight for *Dolphin Tale 2*, CMA needed to contribute $10 million to the effort. Quick, open up another lemonade stand! Even if we were out of the red with all the media attention and the flush of visitors, we weren't exactly flush with cash.

Remember the state film incentives I discussed earlier? When *Dolphin Tale 2* came up, I started monitoring the Florida film incentives pool and found there were no funds available since they were allocated to other TV and film projects around the state. However, after talking to the State Film Commissioner, we applied for any funds that might become available through canceled projects. That occasionally happens, and in such cases, the funds go back to the overall pool for reallocation. It was a long shot, but we applied. Then we waited.

Without that additional funding, the whole sequel dream would be unrealized. Sure enough, after a little while, a project here and there got canceled. Then after a few more months, unbelievably, we were first in line. All we needed was for one more project to cancel. It did. *Were we actually going to pull this off again?* I now had funding to the tune of just over $5 million, and with half of our obligation covered, we were closer to the goal. We needed another $5 million. Ugh, okay. Time to swim a little harder.

The economic impact CMA made on our area was estimated to be in the hundreds of millions of dollars over the years. Former Governor Rick Scott (now US Senator) had come to CMA several times and was a big supporter of tourism (Florida's number-one industry). He heard about our impact on tourism and became one of our greatest advocates. Governor Scott gave me a Governor's Ambassador Award and invited Joan and me to the governor's mansion for dinner.

Our local state legislature delegation got behind a bill that would award us a second $5 million grant. It would come from the regular state budget, which, if approved, would be the second Hollywood first for this movie. All TV and movie incentive funds come from specifically authorized incentive funding pools, not the general state budget.

Working a bill through any state legislature is a major challenge, and they can "die" at any time. I also had a lot of strong currents coming against me— film studios in particular. Studios working in Florida weren't exactly happy that I might get funding from the state, whereas their movies would not. I have to say, it was a logical concern, and I couldn't argue with them. Thus began my foray into politics. It was simple. If they opposed me, that was the ball game.

Press conference – with Senator Rick Scott (then Governor)

The $5 Million Call

The ultimate pressure sales call ... for a mere $5 million and a second movie. I decided to pitch all of the Florida movie studio executives in one organized phone call. I told them if they didn't oppose our funding via their elected officials, the *Dolphin Tale* franchise would continue to be the poster child for why Florida needed more film incentives. In other words, "support me and future Florida film incentives will be far more likely to become a reality due to the large return on investment generated for the state by the *Dolphin Tale* movies." I encouraged them to look long term at this win-win proposition (you know how I like those!). Well ... they agreed, and with no further opposition in the legislature, our bill passed, locking in the remaining $5 million we needed. Nobody thought we could pull it off, but we did.

I'm telling you these details because I want you to see the power of believing, of having enough faith to charge up Kilimanjaro without fear. Few believed we could get the first movie off the ground, much less get a second movie. My point is, your purpose can be much bigger than you think, but will you see it and have the courage to believe when everyone else doubts? I hope you will. If I listened to naysayers and dream killers, the global Dolphin Tale franchise would not exist. What's holding you back from fulfilling your BIG LIFE?

Little old Clearwater Marine Aquarium went from being unknown and insolvent to a global nonprofit powerhouse reaching every country of the world. It wasn't magic; it happened through much hard work and perseverance. Nor was the business plan complicated. I simply used the same approach we used at IRONMAN: have a plan, drive a big vision, tell our story, and get critical partners aligned with us. In the end, hundreds of millions of dollars were invested by our partners, and as they say, "The rest is history." If I didn't believe in the power of Winter's story, who would?

Don't miss your Kilimanjaro experience. Recalculate your life and career and get a big vision of your role as a parent, child, business owner, pastor or teacher. Regardless of where you are on your path, there is a BIG purpose for you. God will supply it, but you have to recognize it. The day we feel we have "arrived" and simply float downstream with the current is the day our lives will begin to fizzle out. We are built to keep dreaming and conquering new mountains. Don't pause, and don't plateau. These are the enemies of progress. As my good friend Bill Potts says, "Good is the enemy of great." He's right. In my case, why stop with one movie? Dream big and go for two—and then a TV show!

Back to the Movies

To remain credible to fans of the first *Dolphin Tale* movie, the same actors who played in the original must play in the sequel, right? Imagine some other actor replacing Mark Hamill in the role of Luke Skywalker. It just wouldn't work. The A-listers in the first *Dolphin Tale,* such as Morgan Freeman, Harry Connick, Jr., Ashley Judd, and Kris Kristofferson, are busy people, so getting them a second time and at the same time seemed an impossible task. Yet it happened.

I remember seeing Harry the first day on the set of *Dolphin Tale 2* at Fort De Soto, a fantastic stretch of beach south of Clearwater. I asked him how he could be here since he was on tour supporting his new Christmas CD and filming a little-known TV show called *American Idol!* He responded that he wouldn't think of missing this. Ashley Judd said the same thing, and so did Morgan Freeman, Cozi Zuehlsdorff, Nathan Gamble, Austin Highsmith and on down the line. Here's why: Actors expect to get paid for their work, but more important than money is their dream to be involved in projects that impact society. Sadly, these projects are a rarity. Films like *Dolphin Tale* transform lives, but they're hard to find. Think of other movies like *Schindler's List* or the more recent *I Can Only Imagine.* Films like these go beyond inspiration. They change lives.

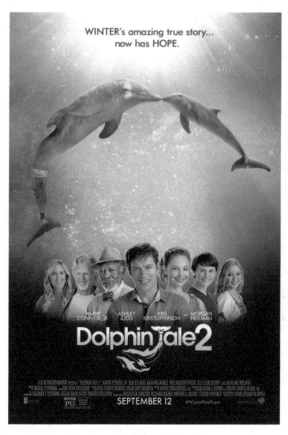

Long story short, having put all the pieces together, we filmed *Dolphin Tale 2*, and it was released in September 2014, three years after the original *Dolphin Tale*. Lightning struck twice. Who would have thought? One movie, you're crazy. Two movies? NO WAY!

Filming a turtle scene in Dolphin Tale 2 *– I'm the skinny guy on the right with the hat*

My daughter Tiffany and Cozi in the middle, with friend Savanna and niece Hanna, at the Dolphin Tale 2 *premiere*

10

WINTER'S BIG LIFE

Zoe's Story

As much as the first movie made an economic and financial impact, and as much as the critics loved it, the real impact was measured in lives. Millions of lives. People can live their entire lives wanting to help others yet not knowing how to do it. I can't tell you all the tears of gratitude those movies produced, the number of people who recommitted to do better, be better, and even fight for their very lives.

I've seen people at the very end of their ropes, hating their very existence, come and see Winter and leave as entirely new people. As potent as the phrase "life-changing" is, it is an apt description of the miraculous change Winter's story has brought about for so many. At the start of filming *Dolphin Tale 2,* the actors and crew had heard about the impact *Dolphin Tale* had made, but they hadn't witnessed it in person. They were about to.

One day, mid-shoot, we got a call from one of the many children's organizations we work with: Make-A-Wish. The caller asked if we could host a young girl and her family from Switzerland. Her name was Zoe. Little Zoe was nearly five years old and had a form of cancer called neuroblastoma. Sadly, she was terminal. Knowing her time was short, her family planned to fly from Switzerland just to see Winter. You see, Winter inspired little Zoe during her cancer treatments by giving her something her young mind could relate to. Her family saw the impact our dolphin had on Zoe and wanted to brighten her world one last time by having her meet Winter before she succumbed to the cancer. The cost for a trip from Switzerland for a family of four to Florida, including a week-long stay at a nice hotel, is not cheap. When I found out their intentions, I figured that cancer cost this family enough. Someone else had to let Zoe know she was loved. With a sense of humility, we jumped at the opportunity to host the family. I still wish I could have seen little Zoe's face when they told her she would meet Winter.

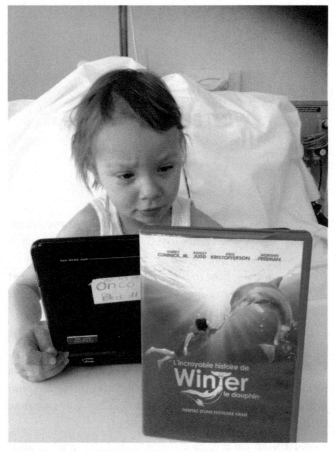

Little Zoe watching Dolphin Tale *over and over again in the hospital*

A few weeks later, they made the pilgrimage to Florida and stayed at the Clearwater Beach Hilton. Since we didn't film on weekends, the plan was for the family to visit on Saturday. At least that was the plan, but cancer tends to change things. We got a call on Wednesday during filming that made us catch our breath. The Clearwater Beach Hilton manager asked on behalf of the family if they could visit that very day because they didn't know if Zoe would live until Saturday. Okay, at this point, it's hard to keep writing. How do I convey the feeling I had when I heard that? It was a dagger through my heart. I can't imagine how her parents felt, knowing their little girl would never ride a bike, kiss a boy, get married, or even live long enough to go to school. I had to be alone for a moment to let my grief out, and it took longer than I expected for someone I had never met. But this little girl had but hours to live, *days at the most.*

While filming a major motion picture, one cardinal rule is: You do not stop filming for anything, ever. Filming is very expensive, and once you get into the workday, you don't stop until the director says, "That's a wrap." There could be a massive earthquake, or Ariana Grande could drop through the roof, but unless the director yells, "Cut!" the cameras keep rolling. But this was bigger than an earthquake, and it would be a first for the cast, the crew and even the director. We went to him and explained what was happening. With grace and understanding, he immediately agreed to stop filming to let Zoe meet Winter.

Another thing about making a movie is that hundreds of off-screen crew-members perform all kinds of roles during the shooting. Camera operators, producers, set design teams, production assistants and audio technicians all have a role in production. I said it before, but I'll say it again: shutting down production is a huge deal.

When the crew was told about Zoe and what was about to happen, every-thing went quiet; there was a collective feeling of reverence. The atmosphere inexplicably changed, like we were receiving a fresh current of warm air. As the crew stood back, all eyes were respectfully on Zoe and her family when they walked into the filming area. I paced in nervous anticipation, hoping with all my might that it would be a sacred moment for the family. After all, there was no way to explain to Winter the severity of the moment; at times, she would get excited and playful, while at other times, she could seem standoffish. But if any-one ever needed a win, it was now. I whispered to myself, "Come on, Winter, I need you to be great right now. I need you to help this little girl."

Four-year-old Zoe was so sick that she had to be carried by her mother while her father and her eight-year-old sister followed behind. Her mother, a force of love and determination, brought her daughter onto the platform to get close to Winter as we looked on, holding our breath in anticipation. Tears be-gan to flow as Zoe's dream was being fulfilled before our eyes. Soft sobs escaped into the quietness.

One of our dolphin caregivers who spoke their language talked to the fam-ily while Zoe's mom lowered her sick little body so she would be able to touch Winter with her toes. The moment was too intense for me, so I shifted my gaze from Zoe as Winter approached and took in the entire scene. I marveled at the absolute respect and sympathy everyone had for this hurting family. I think it's fair to say that few who witnessed that event had ever experienced a more powerful, emotionally raw moment in their lives. Zoe's mom and dad openly wept as all the pent-up emotion of the trip, and probably the last four years, poured out. I will never forget the image of Zoe being held so she could touch Winter, even though she could not control her legs. Winter played the role of hero perfectly. She snuggled with the sick little Zoe and chattered with her as if she felt her distress.

Thirty minutes later and tender with emotion, the family made their way off the platform, smiling through tears. When I got close to Zoe, I could see how very weak and limp her little body was. The family lingered to talk for a few minutes and then thanked everyone with humility and softness. Most could just smile and nod in gratitude for being allowed to share in what might have been their most intimate moment. When they headed back to the hotel, we were all left with a "what do we do now?" feeling. How could we go back to shooting after that? The rest of the day was a blur as the cast and crew tried to digest what they had just seen. I experienced this many times, but they had not.

Two days later, Zoe passed away.

You may wonder why it was so important for Zoe and her family to travel to CMA with Zoe near death. The answer came on Saturday when I was in my office. One of my team said Zoe's family was at the front gate and wanted to speak with me. I froze. Why would they be here the day after their child had died? Was there an issue? Troubling thoughts ran through my head as I wondered if we had done something to offend them.

I walked to the front gate where Zoe's mom, dad and sister waited. Through broken English, they said they came back to thank me for giving Zoe the final experience of her life. They captured the last memory they had hoped for with their little Zoe. This memory would be for a lifetime. They said Winter meant the world to Zoe, and they had hoped against hope that she would get to meet her hero before she passed. "We will never forget the kindness you showed our daughter," they said. We were all in tears. Two years later, the family returned to CMA on the anniversary of Zoe's death to celebrate her life and the memory of that moment. Staff members that were present when Zoe was there, and those who had heard about it, treated them like royalty. There were many more smiles and laughter that day … "Just as Zoe would have wanted it," her mother said.

Zoe's Family at CMA

Zoe's story evokes the kind of emotion that lives in every human being. What still amazes me is how the tragic end of her life had been softened by the affections of a 275-pound marine mammal. As remarkable as Zoe's story is, it is just one of the countless stories that demonstrate Winter's remarkable ability to impart strength and inspiration to all who came to know her. Zoe indeed led a BIG LIFE in her few short years.

Never, ever underestimate the power of inspiration.

Oh, the Letters

When the first *Dolphin Tale* movie came out, we were inundated with thousands upon thousands of letters, calls and social media posts telling us of their personal Winter connection story. We received over 10,000 emails on opening weekend alone! Did you catch that? That three-day window was how long it took for Winter's story to start taking hold of the world via the movie. Even before the film, we had begun to host families impacted by Winter. Now, though we were buried in all those queries, we committed to responding to every one because we knew each contained a life-changing story. When I first began telling Winter's story, it was to raise awareness of CMA and our educational mission. Once I saw the life-changing impact Winter brought to so many, it became a responsibility to keep telling her story. I knew that every time I did, lives would be changed. Who gets an opportunity like that?

For Winter

for inspiring me
and making winter
the love of my
life
        -Love
        Julia

WinteR
YOU ARE
In
MY
heaRt

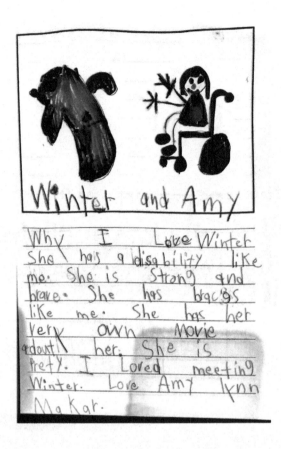

Winter and Amy

Why I Love Winter
She has a disability like
me. She is strong and
brave. She has braces
like me. She has her
very own Movie
about her. She is
pretty. I Loved meeting
Winter. Love Amy lynn
Ma Kar.

Are you just getting through the day with no sense of a more significant reason to be alive? Believe that you were born for something greater. Beautiful souls like Zoe have been taken from us far too early. Yet you are still here. The story of your life, of which you are the greatest contributor, has not yet been finished. You were born to create, build, write, help, restore and positively impact your generation and the world. I urge you to start looking inside yourself today. What pulls at you? What breaks your heart? Who can you help? If you don't search yourself to find your greatness, you'll never have a sense of fulfillment regardless of how much money you make or your standing in society.

The Bible tells us in the book of Mark that we can "… gain the whole world but lose our soul." That's a striking and disruptive statement. What does it mean? It means that life is more than just making money. You can have outward success with business, finance, social standing, a ballooning retirement *portfolio and even have a street named after you. Still, you can be bankrupt in your soul because you missed your purpose and lived for yourself instead of for God and others.*

Pas·sion /ˈpa SHən/: strong and barely controllable emotion.

Your life will be miserable without passion. Let it guide you through your BIG LIFE. The dictionary defines passion as a "strong and barely controllable emotion." Live that way. How many mountains were climbed without passion? How many miracles of modern medicine were accomplished without passion? Can you imagine the Apollo 11 crew making it to the moon without NASA's passion? You get the point.

"For where your treasure is, there your heart will be also."

~ Matthew 6:21

FaceTimes and Hospital Visits

After *Dolphin Tale* came out, I invited Cozi, Nathan and Austin back to CMA for promotional efforts, including autograph and picture sessions with our CMA guests. Whenever they were present, huge lines formed to meet these inspiring and humble actors. I often FaceTimed when they were not at CMA with sick or injured kids who came to CMA for their Winter "pilgrimage." Now, you would think that a little FaceTime isn't much, but consider this: Cozi is, among other things, a Disney star (*Liv and Maddie, Mighty Med, KC Undercover* and the lead role of Ellie in the 2018 remake of *Freaky Friday*); Nathan has acted with Brad Pitt (*Babel*), Heath Ledger (*The Dark Knight*) and Owen Wilson and Jennifer Aniston (*Marley and Me*); and Austin has appeared on too many TV shows to list (*Hawaii Five-O, CSI, Private Practice* and *Criminal Minds* to name just a few). As she puts it, she either "cried or died" on many of them. These three actors are heroes to Winter fans.

Nathan Gamble FaceTiming Autism Overcomer Aurora Post

Cozi Zuehlsdorff and Austin Highsmith FaceTiming Autism Overcomer Devon Jones

You would think they'd all have enormous egos, but it's precisely the opposite. Every time these three came to town, it was standard protocol to hit the local children's hospital to visit sick kids. On one of our many visitations, Austin experienced a "life moment." In her children's book, *The Miracle Tree*, Austin chronicles how she nearly died from an eye infection that required emergency surgery to save her at age two. Fast-forward to when we walked into a hospital room and met a young girl suffering from the very same condition. It took a bit of coaxing for the girl to explain her situation. It was as if she was embarrassed because she wasn't normal. When she did, Austin said, "That's exactly what I had when I was about your age." It looked as if the girl didn't believe it. Here was a beautiful film star telling her that she had the same problem when she was about the same age. The girl shied away and looked down as if ashamed. Austin leaned into her. "I did. Look at me, please." The girl picked her head up. "I had the same thing and look at me now."

Austin, reading her book to attentive listeners at CMA with the help of Nathan Gamble. Can be purchased at DoceBlantstore.com under Austin Highsmith.

Sadly, I had seen the look on that little girl's face many times before. She seemed afraid to hope. I sensed a struggle going on in her little head as if she was thinking, *Could this be true? Could this lady from the movies be just like me?*

The young girl's mother confirmed my suspicion when she spoke up, feeling the need to back Austin up. "Sweetie, it's true. And now look at how beautiful Austin is!"

A lump stuck in my throat. "Oh my goodness," Austin said with much emotion. "Yes, sweetie. Yes, you are beautiful, and you're going to live a great life!" That was it. We all began to tear up. As we walked out of the room, the emotional moment hit Austin head-on. She broke down, remembering how she'd felt as a two-year-old in a strange hospital world. Austin saw herself in that little girl. In return, the girl received a massive dose of hope that day, medicine better than anything the doctors could have given her at that moment.

More Inspiration

As I mentioned, we have thousands upon thousands of families telling us how Winter's overcoming story transformed their child's life. I've had the awesome privilege of connecting with many of them myself. One day I received this email:

> *Dear CMA,*
>
> *My name is Hannah, and I am twenty years old. I am disabled. I was a healthy child until I started getting pain when I was 12 and needed my appendix out. My appendix was healthy, but I had stones pushing into it that caused my pain. I've had pain ever since, and the situation progressed from me not being able to do physical education at school to now being unable to walk properly. I can now only just hobble a few steps, and so I use a power chair scooter. I live on morphine and spend most of my days in bed, drugged up and screaming out in pain.*
>
> *I went to Mexico in the early stages of my condition, where I was with dolphins, and it was just amazing because I finally felt a connection with something that could be a potential career. I soon developed an obsession with marine life, especially dolphins. One day, I found the film Dolphin Tale and watched it. It truly touched me, but the main part was at the end when I saw footage that proved the story was based on fact, and it just really connected with me.*
>
> *After that, I just became in love with Winter. I did want to rescue stranded marine life like in the film, but I am now physically unable to. I am now working towards a biological science degree and then going on to a marine biology postgraduate degree with the plan of*

working as someone who will examine marine mammals and design prosthetic limbs for them.

However, my pain has now reached the point that I honestly don't think I can live like this much longer, and I have decided that if the situation does not improve, I will be euthanized by the age of 25. Watching Winter online and knowing her story has been one of the only things (alongside my parents, brothers, and dog) to get me through this difficult time. I love her so, so much, and I couldn't bear the thought of not meeting her before I die. The pain can only be described as though you are being attacked with a knife over and over again. The medication doesn't give me relief for very long, and I barely sleep due to the pain. I'm just exhausted. I know my condition isn't fatal, but this is getting worse, and that petrifies me, and I just can't live like this for the next fifty years.

Please, I beg you, I know you must get many emails like this, but please help me to fulfill this wish before I have to end my life.

Kind regards,

Hannah Wood, UK

I lost my breath. It didn't seem fair. Hannah was blindsided by a life of pain, sorrow, despair and hopelessness. The pain was so bad she was willing to take her own life. I couldn't imagine the conversation she must have had with her parents about her willingness to die.

Is there a greater purpose on Earth than to help save someone's life? Game on. I had to make a plan that would help Hannah stay alive. We had to provide her with a reason to live. Hannah made her first visit to CMA with her parents in March 2018, and we rolled out the red carpet. Hannah was the official CMA VIP that day. Her visit with Winter was just as important to Hannah and her family as it had been for Zoe and her family, except it was different. It was fun, splashy, and loud. She was so encouraged by being around Winter that she told me she wanted to work at CMA someday. Hearing this, I made her a deal. I told her if she stayed positive, worked with her doctors, and finished school that she would have a job waiting for her at CMA. We shook on it. In the meantime, she had medical issues that could not be ignored. Her pain was real, and she was on a morphine drip most days.

Since Hannah is from the UK, she and her family rely on their socialized medical system. After years of walking down a long road of medical procedures, nothing seemed to work. I kept hoping for good news from the family, but it never came. Her last and best chance was a procedure called a "DRG," but it would take years for her to be considered for approval if she was approved at all. Without insurance, the procedure would cost around $30,000 US, something no middle-class family could afford. When I heard this, it was time to go beyond just inspiring her. We needed to fundraise for her and put our efforts where our hearts were. With Winter and CMA's help, we raised funds, and we sent $20,000 to her for the procedure. It came just in the nick of time. Hannah is progressing as I write this, and we keep in touch regularly. Her mother (mum) sent me this note, which I'll forever cherish.

Hi David,

Thank you so much for the money towards Hannah's treatment. In fact, you have paid for the majority of it! We feel so privileged to have you in our lives. I've always felt from the moment I met you that you are like a guardian angel to Hannah. I know when my time comes to leave this world, you will guide her forward. We have the exact amount of funds for the treatment. We will be eternally grateful to you for all your support, both financially and spiritually. You have restored Hannah's faith in God, and as I've said to you before, all the signs we have been experiencing of late have given us such a positive feeling I just can't put into words. It's been exhausting and a very long journey of suffering. We Thank God you have been there for us.

Love, Julie

That, my friends, gives me purpose. More than I thought I would ever have. What is your purpose? Find your Hannah and change a life.

Bob, Hannah and Julie

Anni's Story: A New Arm Meets a New Tail

Dear David,

Thank You for everything you have done for not only me but for all of the other children you have brought to the aquarium. Knowing that there is a person out there who would do anything for others who are different gives me courage. David Yates, you are my Superhero!

Love,

Anni Emmert

Anni's letter was in the opening of this book. Annika "Anni" Emmert was born with a congenital disability that prevented her right arm and hand from fully developing. Now, if kids tend to bully fully functioning kids, imagine how cruel they can be to someone with a physical issue. But Anni is a fighter, and she refused to hide in her house. There was too much to live for.

Anni and her family heard about a team of students from the University of Central Florida. The team, led by a student named Albert Manero, made prosthetics for kids using 3-D printing, and they did it for free. One day my son Chris called and said Albert Manero was trying to reach me. We knew the Manero family; we had attended the same church a few years before. When I called him, Albert told me he had an idea. Anni was a big *Dolphin Tale* and Winter fan, and he had just engineered a prosthetic arm for her. "Why not surprise her with the arm during a visit to CMA?" Albert suggested.

I answered wholeheartedly, "Why not, indeed!" Then I began to plot.

On June 5, 2015, Anni and her family arrived at CMA with Anni thinking she was simply going to visit her hero, Winter. Here's where it got exciting: as if meeting Winter wasn't a big enough deal for little Anni, we had worked it out to have ABC's *Good Morning America* there to film the whole thing. To top it off, none other than Cozi Zuehlsdorff (Hazel in the *Dolphin Tale* movies) was also there to escort her onto the platform to meet Winter!

But Anni had yet another surprise coming after she got over the wonderful shock of meeting Winter and Cozi. While on the platform in front of Winter, she was asked to open a cooler that supposedly held fish for Winter. "No way! Do I really get to feed Winter?" she squealed with delight. Then she paused, probably wondering how she would grab the fish with her one good arm. When Anni opened the cooler, she gazed inside for several long moments. A few others and I knew what was in it, but she had no idea what was waiting inside.

"Is that for me?" she cried out in disbelief. Nestled inside the cooler was her unique new prosthetic arm! Breaking out in tears, she pulled out the arm and showed it off to everyone around, much like a child showing off a fantastic Christmas gift. She put on her new arm, right in front of the curiously watching Winter. They both loved it! She had a cool new arm, something the bullies didn't have.

Today, Anni is a beautiful young lady and leads an active, productive life and visits CMA, often bringing others to be inspired. "They've literally changed her life," her mom said. "I am speechless."

Anni gets her new arm – Surprise!

Ellie Frodsham's Story: From Surgery to the Red Carpet

Ellie Frodsham was born with a short femur bone in her right leg. At age three and then five, she'd had two failed surgeries to try to fix her hip. Feeling helpless and hopeless, her parents were advised to let the surgeons amputate Ellie's leg. While considering this, they heard about an amazing limb lengthening orthopedic specialist in Florida, and as a last hope, they contacted him. A few weeks before seeing that doctor in Florida, Ellie watched *Dolphin Tale*, and after seeing the movie, she pleaded with her parents, "Can we visit Winter the Dolphin when we go to Florida to meet the doctor?" They said yes.

Upon arrival at CMA, Ellie couldn't wait to see Winter, her real-life hero. After all, she and Winter had similar issues. As her mom explained:

> *"It was such a memorable moment for her that she will never forget! It helped Ellie to restore hope that things would work out someday. She saw how this dolphin went through hard times and never gave up, so it gave her the courage and strength to continue with the hope that we would find a doctor to help her leg. Ellie thought, if Winter can, then I can too! Seeing Winter always gives Ellie a sense of peace and calmness before she has to go to the hospital for surgeries."*

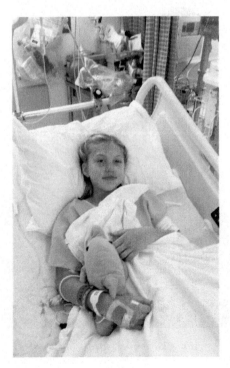

I had another idea about how to inspire this young fighter, and her mother wrote about it:

"Another exciting thing happened when Ellie was recovering from her first limb lengthening surgery. David Yates gave Ellie a challenge and told her that if she worked hard to walk without crutches, then she would be able to walk on the 'Blue' Carpet with the stars and see the movie premiere of Dolphin Tale 2 in Los Angeles."

Ellie added:

"As a child, Winter had inspired me to do the impossible and be my best self. After I had been recovering from a pretty successful limb lengthening surgery, David challenged me to get off my crutches and learn how to walk again, and in return, he would bring me as a guest to the Dolphin Tale 2 premiere. That was such an exciting invitation for me, and it motivated me to work so hard on rehabilitating my leg to make it to walk on the 'Blue' Carpet with all the Stars."

Ellie worked incredibly hard fighting off disappointments and setbacks, but there she is, front and center in this picture, on the Blue Carpet (we used blue instead of red for an ocean look).

Sometimes, all someone needs is a reason to fight on.

A Dolphin and a Soldier

In the early days, even as Winter's story traveled worldwide, inspiring millions of children, I was unsure how much her story would connect with older age groups. Then, in September 2007, when Winter had been with us less than a year, I received a letter (or should I say Winter received a letter) from a group of wounded veterans. They were associated with the James P. Haley Veterans Administration in Tampa, just across the bay from CMA.

Specifically, the letter was from a group called AVAST, or Amputee Veterans Administration Support Team. They were people who answered the call when their country needed them. Unfortunately, these heroes lost limbs in a war zone. They heard about Winter's inspirational story and couldn't help but make the connection. Think of it; these were full-grown, battle-hardened soldiers, and yet Winter had melted their hearts as well. That is proof that the human heart never truly grows old.

AVAST
AMPUTEE VA SUPPORT TEAM
TAMPA, FLORIDA

SEPTEMBER 1, 2007

DEAR WINTER,

LET ME START BY INTRODUCING OURSELVES, WE ARE AVAST, AN AMPUTEE SUPPORT TEAM AT THE TAMPA VA MEDICAL CENTER. OUR TEAM IS MADE UP OF VETERANS WITH VARIOUS AMPUTATIONS, THEIR FAMILY MEMBERS, FRIENDS AND VA MEDICAL CENTER STAFF. THE FUNCTION OF THE TEAM IS TO LEND SUPPORT TO ALL MEMBERS WHO MAY NEED OUR ASSISTANCE.

WE WERE VERY INTRIGUED BY YOUR STORY AND THE COURAGE YOU HAVE DEMONSTRATED. AS WE TELL ALL OF OUR AMPUTEES, LEARN TO LIVE WITH THE BODY YOU HAVE NOW, DON'T RUSH DURING YOUR REHAB PROCESS. ALL LIVING THINGS HAVE THEIR OWN PACE OF RECOVERY.

ENCLOSED YOU WILL FIND ONE OF OUR SHIRTS, MAKING YOU AN HONORARY MEMBER OF OUR TEAM. YOUR WILL TO SURVIVE IS AN INSPIRATION TO US ALL. WE AS AMPUTEE VETERNS AND FELLOW TEAM MEMBERS SALUTE AND THANK YOU. DON'T FORGET WE ARE BEHIND YOU 100%.

SINCERELY,

ROBERT WEST
AVAST CHAIRMAN

That wasn't just another letter that touched me and made me smile. It was much more than that. I saw another opportunity to further my purpose by reaching out to those veterans. If we went out of our way to help those who suffered an illness or accident, how could we not do the very least for those men and women who signed up voluntarily to defend our freedoms with their lives? Sadly, the cost of liberty is terrible and made evident by the many traumatic and lifelong injuries our soldiers have sustained. I felt honored and privileged, so I contacted the program's local director at the VA hospital in Tampa. I wanted to know more about how and why they connected to Winter's story the same way so many kids have done.

So I met with Jim Switzer, the program manager, and over lunch, we developed a program to bring wounded soldiers to CMA any time they needed inspiration. That was significant because that particular VA gets quite a few traumatic brain injury (TBI) soldiers as patients. Soon after we met, Jim called and said there was a wounded soldier he wanted us to meet. Hopefully, we could impart some inspiration into his life. His name was Staff Sergeant Russell Marek, or "Russ."

Russ was a tank commander in Iraq in 2005. His tank hit an IED, immediately killing two of his fellow soldiers. Russ survived, but just barely. The shrapnel hit the right side of his body, and he lost part of his right arm and right leg.

His left arm and left leg were intact, but since the blast was to the right side, the concussion to the right side of the brain caused him to lose control over some of the left side of his body. He was in a coma for 52 days at Walter Reed Hospital in Maryland, and his long-term survival was in doubt. He wasn't sure he wanted to live. They transferred Russ to Tampa because of his traumatic brain injury. It was shortly after that when Jim Switzer called.

We were honored to host Russ and his mother, Rose, at CMA. Admittedly, though, I had only just begun to work with individuals with medical issues like this, and I didn't know what to expect. I wondered how we could host adults with significant injuries, including those having suffered major brain trauma. We were pioneering new territory, but we were up to the task and determined to find a way to help heroes like this.

After Russ and his mom arrived, I took them into one of our conference rooms and began to share Winter's story. Russ couldn't speak well at that time, so he didn't respond. I wanted so badly to reach him, to give him hope, so I told the story with as much emotion as possible.

Still, he didn't respond. After that, we helped him down onto the dolphin platform to spend face-to-face time with Winter while we attached her new prosthetic tail. At the time, Russ was also being fitted with a prosthetic for one of his arms, and he struggled with it. When he watched Winter and her new prosthetic, he could see how she struggled as well.

The whole time Russ was at CMA, we didn't know what was going on in his mind. He used a walker to get around but didn't say much, so I wasn't sure whether we had connected with him or not. Well, a few days later, his mom called back and explained what had happened. Russ told her that he saw how Winter struggled to wear her prosthetic tail and exclaimed, "If that dolphin can use prosthetics, WELL THEN SO CAN I!" And that is how the bumper sticker was born "If Winter can, I can." The dolphin and the soldier had connected. Unlike many areas of life, hope doesn't fall into a generation gap, a financial gap, a racial gap, or a political gap. Hope transcends all of those man-made things. Since that time, Russ calls Winter his "dolphin role model."

Russ and the family have since become dear friends. His life has moved ahead dramatically to the point that he has skydived, gives motivational talks, and has brought other wounded soldiers to CMA. Russ has a caring family around him. He's a superb example of how never giving up is the answer. He learned that firsthand from a little dolphin. Russ continues to lead his own BIG LIFE. As for me, I was excited we had found an entirely new avenue in which to inspire our military heroes. We would dive deep into that area in the coming years. What an honor.

Russ (right) and another wounded soldier with Winter

The statistics are heartbreaking. Every day, 22 soldiers commit suicide in America. *That is every single day.* Russ was of the same mindset. Imagine being young and healthy, feeling like the world is your oyster, only to lose an arm, a leg, the use of most of your left side and a brain injury on top of it all. It's no wonder soldiers with similar or even worse injuries (not to mention PTSD) contemplate taking their own lives. But then Russ met Winter, and after just one visit, his mindset was completely rejuvenated. He started to work harder with his prosthetics, realizing that just like Winter, he too could have a BIG LIFE despite his injuries. Hope truly is a powerful thing.

To all of our brave soldiers, thank you for being courageous enough to join our military and thank you for your service. Please, don't give up. If you need help, call the Suicide Prevention Hotline in your county. Help is a call away. In the US, call 800-273-8255. Never, ever forget, you are a hero, and you're not alone.

And Then There Are the Heartbreaks

There is a scripture in the Bible that tells us to "rejoice with those who re-joice; mourn with those who mourn" (Romans 12:15). My work has connected me with those who have miraculous overcoming stories and with those who, despite their boundless courage, have succumbed. I have rejoiced, and I have wept, and I have seen the surpassing beauty that encompasses both outcomes. Here is just one example of a life that touched my life profoundly.

Rebecca Neu – From her mom as written to me, asking for a visit with Winter:

> "Rebecca was diagnosed with Friedreich's Ataxia when she was seven years old, and by the time she was 12, she was permanently wheel-chair-bound. Over the years, she won the genetic lottery and added a heart condition, scoliosis, and diabetes to the mix. Against the odds, Rebecca has graduated high school and even completed two semesters of college. Over the last year, she has battled serious depression. In wanting to live her life to the fullest, she decided to seek professional help in the hopes that she could move forward with her dream of becoming a Teacher's Assistant and working with children.
>
> Something happened, however, to change those plans. Sometime over the course of eight days in a treatment program, Becky ended

up in cardiac failure. After being transferred to a Cardiac ICU, we found that she was in full heart, kidney, and liver failure and we were advised to call our family to say goodbye. Two days and 100 people later, Becky's strength showed up once again and she started to pull through. Against all odds, we are home again a month later, and we have been given a second chance to make her life special. Unfortunately, irreparable damage was done, and we are now in month two of a six-month prognosis."

Rebecca died four days after this picture. Rest in peace, dear warrior.

11

MULTIPLYING THE BLESSINGS

After the experience with Army veteran Russ Marek, I realized Winter's story was becoming much bigger, and I had some pretty big dreams for it already. As we humbly hosted more and more wounded soldiers, it amazed me how they could maintain such incredibly positive attitudes after their terrible injuries. I recall one vet who was completely blinded by an explosion, and nearly half of his skull was gone. He sat in my office one afternoon and told me how great things were with his life. Crazy.

Millions of us complain about the smallest inconveniences, even a little thing like having to pump the brakes when someone pulls out in front of us. We complain about coffee not being hot enough and water not being cold enough. We get ticked off when the Wi-Fi resets or when we are forced to wait ten seconds to continue binge-watching the next Netflix episode while seated on a reclining leather sofa in a climate-controlled room! We allow one little thing to anger us. Trust me, I do too. We allow inconveniences to make us forget how great we have it. When people survive tragedies like those I've shared and still live with joy and come out on top, it humbles me. I've learned some great life lessons being around these guys and gals.

My Dreams and My Purposes Converge

Over the years, my dreams and my purposes have converged. As CEO of both IRONMAN and CMA, and as a producer of the *Dolphin Tale* movies, I've worked with thousands of kids with disabilities at CMA and hundreds of disabled athletes at IRONMAN. Honoring the military was also a big part of what we did at IRONMAN, so as I expanded the wounded soldiers' program at CMA, I felt the desire to take the next step and work with Gold Star families—those who have lost a family member in our country's service.

Matthew Sitton's Story

Talk about a BIG LIFE. Matthew Sitton attended a local private school and was in the same grade as my oldest son, Joshua, who attended another nearby private school. Matthew and Joshua both played sports and probably competed against each other more than once, although they didn't know each other. After a short stint in college, Matthew joined the Army and rose in the ranks to become a strong young leader in the Afghanistan deployment. When he was about to return to the States, he conversed with his young wife, Sarah, about their newborn son, Brodey. He told her for the millionth time how much he missed his little boy and how phone calls weren't enough. He couldn't wait to pick up his son. They spoke about how much fun Brodey would have at CMA and picked the date they would come. That never happened. A few days later, while on foot patrol, Matthew's first sergeant stepped on an IED, and both he and Matthew were killed. Just like that, Matthew—a husband, father, brother and son—was gone in a second. There were no goodbyes. Young Brodey would never again see his father.

Matthew's funeral was a big deal, as it should have been. The entire Tampa community mourned the loss of a real hero. One of our board members called and told me about Matthew, saying he was in contact with the family. We talked and came up with the idea to invite the Sitton family to CMA to host a "Matthew Sitton Day." We would donate some of the ticket sales to help Matthew do what he was no longer able to do: pay for Brodey's future education.

We did, and that day in September of 2012 is burned into my memory. Getting to meet the family and young Brodey was much more impactful than I had expected. Just watching the happy and curious boy jump around CMA, followed by his mom, who had lost her husband in a flash in defense of our country, tore at my heart. It turned out to be one of the most emotional days I have ever lived through.

Matthew's mother, Cheryl Sitton, wife, Sarah, and son, Brodey,
meeting Winter weeks after Matthew's death

The Sitton family are now dear friends. At the Clearwater premiere of *Dolphin Tale 2*, I decided to honor and surprise them. Matthew's mom, Cheryl, described the night in a Facebook post:

> *"As most of you know, I am an 'occasional' poster. There has to be an occasion for me to post. Last night we had the incredible privilege to be invited to the premiere of Dolphin Tale 2 (which was terrific). As we were coming down the stairs to the main floor, Cody notices a guy with a shirt that says, 'Team Matthew Sitton.' As we got closer, Jessy sees that a lot of people had it on. We get down to the main floor and find the entire Clearwater Marine Aquarium staff have them on. Took my breath away!*

Then they ask us to go behind the stage, and David Yates, the CEO, calls us out on stage to allow the audience to honor and thank Matty. Then David announces collection boxes at each door to go towards Brodey's college/trust fund. Are you kidding me! God, you are so AMAZING, and we are humbled, and in awe of the incredible blessing you continue to pour out. Thank you, CMA, and all the precious staff. We love you! And all our Facebook friends, please go see the movie and support these awesome folks."

There were 2,200 people at the premiere. When they heard the emotional story of Matthew Sitton's untimely death, they all rose to their feet as the tears fell. A wave of appreciation and love covered the hall in a way most people will never forget. Matthew had run the good race. He lived his own BIG LIFE. In a sad twist of fate, one of Matthew's high school buddies had died in Afghanistan just a year before. Two young men from the same high school chasing life and serving God had been taken too soon. Godspeed to both Matthew Sitton and Frank Gross.

Life is about helping others. Your experiences, efforts, time, compassion, and kindness are meant to be shared. The earlier we figure that out, the sooner we'll get to our BIG LIFE.

Sitton Family, Cozi and Nathan at Dolphin Tale 2 *Premiere*

Working with Gold Star Families

It was February 6, 2016. Before I walked through the door, I paused. I knew that every set of eyes I was about to look into would be a mother or father who had lost a son or daughter in service to our country. Part of me hoped the room would be empty and that there would be no parents there who had gone through the terrible ordeal of burying their children. But that was not the case. Inside the room, Gold Star moms from across the Tampa area were holding one of their regular meetings at CMA, and I was honored to host them. The result filled me with the desire to honor Gold Star families whenever and wherever I could. It became another life calling for me. I found another purpose, and I was going full-on. Those men, women, and families we honored didn't deserve any less.

Then I had heard about the great work the Gary Sinise Foundation is doing with Gold Star families. Under the banner of "The Snowball Express," the foundation flies Gold Star families to Disney World every year for a few days of free fun and inspiration. When the families emerge from the plane, they board buses and are escorted by a colorful caravan of veterans on motorcycles. Upon arrival at their Disney hotel, they are met by cheerleaders and local high school bands before checking in. The event creates a moment in time when the families are treated like the heroes they are. It's another incredibly emotional experience.

We were invited to be involved in the Snowball Express in December of 2018 in Orlando. Our involvement, of course, was via Winter's story. We had previously worked with a young girl named Autumn Swank. Autumn has brain cancer and, at the young age of 14, had decided she wanted to help Gold Star kids by giving them each a plush animal at the Snowball Express events, inspired to do so by seeing a boy in a nearby hospital room who had no toys in his room. I heard what she had done and that she was a *Dolphin Tale* fan, so we brought her to CMA for what she thought was a simple visit. What she didn't know was that we had organized a major event, and when she pulled up to CMA with her family, we had hundreds lined up to greet her, including local police and first responders. I announced that we would help her get thousands of plush animals donated for the campaign. And that's what we did. Then came the day to hand them out at Snowball Express. Wow, what a day.

Autumn Surprised at CMA

My head of marketing, Bill Potts, and I personally handed out Winter plush dolls to hundreds of Gold Star kids as they entered the hotel, and in the process, we met many of them. It was sobering. I realized every one of them had lost a mother or father in battle. It was difficult to hold myself together. Everyone present was in tears as we watched young children pour out of the buses by the hundreds. It was too much. I had to turn away at one point as I didn't want the kids to see anything but happiness. You couldn't meet the eyes of that many Gold Star kids and maintain your composure. I couldn't. The sheer volume of the tragedy that this many people were living through hit me like a brick wall.

What I didn't quite expect was how hard it would be for me to meet the spouses. Each one had a unique but somehow similar story of marrying someone honorable and selfless, creating a family with him or her, and then tragically losing them, forcing them to go through the rest of life alone as single parents. I could only imagine the void in their hearts! I just wanted to hug every one of them and tell them that things would get better.

One of the wonderful results of this gathering was that, for the first time, many of these children and spouses found others walking through the same life journey. They had shouldered this heavy burden on their own, never knowing anyone who could understand their pain. They had heard the news alone, told their kids alone, and tucked their children into bed, alone. I saw teen girls forge friendships in a minute, meeting a new friend bonded by grief but ending in a special, lifelong sisterhood. It was *powerful* to see these teenage girls hugging each other with this unexpected comfort.

For all, the experience was therapeutic—even cathartic; powerful, to say the least. Half of the people who cried didn't cry for their loss; they cried for someone else's loss. What filled me with hope was watching people connect. They had finally found someone else who could walk with them. Wow, what a day! God bless Gary Sinise, Amber Johnson and the entire crew. And they do other events like this year-round. What a purpose!

The weekend provided great activities for the families. Most of the activities were happy ones, but a few were quite somber. One in particular was a "flag room" where names of every soldier who sacrificed their life were inscribed below a flag. As the families walked through the room, they were surrounded by over 1,500 flags, and each one had a loved one's name on it. I felt I had entered hallowed ground. As hard as that was, I was stunned to find several flags with two names on them. *Those families had lost two members.*

The foundation also created a wall similar to the Vietnam Memorial in Washington, DC, where the names of all the fallen mothers and fathers were inscribed. Just when I thought I'd regained my composure, I fell apart again. As I walked by this wall for the first time, I saw a young girl taking a picture of her fallen dad's name. Too much …

I will never experience anything more humbling and powerful than those few moments. To all servicemen and women, may God bless you for your service.

New Bumper Sticker: If Gary Sinise Can, I Can!

I was so moved by the Gary Sinise Foundation that I offered to do the same thing at Clearwater Marine Aquarium. On September 21, 2019, we hosted our first Snowball Express event at CMA. We brought in 49 Florida-based Gold Star families for a full day of free activities and food. They arrived in chartered trolley cars to a parade led by a local high school marching band. The excitement and emotions were off the charts. We all felt the magnitude of what we were doing and did our absolute best. Every team member went out of their way to make every person feel as special as they are. While we walked along with the families, emotions were supercharged. The indomitable power of the human spirit was on full display. I still remember the feeling.

As part of the event, we set up our own flag room as they had done in Orlando, and we also added a poster board where they could write notes to their loved ones. Any of us who read the notes wept. It wasn't about a dolphin or any one family. It was about deep sorrow and loss amid a sense of a profoundly appreciative community. My staff and I were humbled that day, honoring those who had lived BIG LIVES.

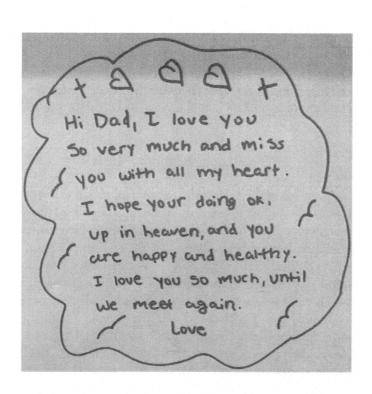

My life started as a disaster, and maybe yours did too. No matter where you are in life now, you still have a BIG LIFE waiting. At the end of the day— or by the end of life, even—everyone's purpose should include a hefty dose of living for and inspiring others. That is especially true in connection with those who cannot do anything to help you in return. That is what I've strived to do.

Hope Fulfilled

As the dolphin "co-star" of *Dolphin Tale 2*, Hope's fame skyrocketed. She became known as the younger "sister" of Winter and developed her own worldwide following. Hope brought her own hope to kids and overcomers. Winter and Hope's relationship has been hilarious to watch over the years, especially in the early days of their relationship. Winter always wanted Hope to know she is the boss, and Hope is like, "Can we just play?" Hope has a propensity to get distracted and is the first to see a guest at a viewing window. She's a real "people person, uh dolphin," loving to show off and just have fun. And why not? This little orphaned dolphin has earned it. Hope fought through her own struggles, and with Winter's help, is now inspiring millions with her own BIG LIFE. After all, I didn't name her Hope for nothing!

Winter & Hope, Delivering Hope

12

IN THE FINAL ANALYSIS

My two most significant career positions have shared one compelling similarity. That is no accident; it's evidence of God's providence in my life. Both IRONMAN and *Dolphin Tale* were about inspiring people to dream big, do more, cast aside doubts, and ignore the naysayers. I didn't write this book to be a cool life story; I wrote it as an account to help you alter *your* life trajectory. After all, if an accountant with a troubled childhood can do this, *what can't you do?* My role at IRONMAN lit the fire of my purpose in inspiring people. Then, when I started at CMA, I found a way to continue and even expand that purpose. What came out of it is the simple, profound message of hope told in a new way. And tell it I did!

Family Is Forever

When you have a busy career that includes traveling worldwide, it can be hard on your family life. Thankfully, I've been blessed with the galaxy's number-one wife, Joan, and four awesome kids—Joshua, Chris, Jordan, and Tiffany—who have put up with Dad's busyness and Type AAAAAAAA personality. In the *Dolphin Tale* movie, a saying is written on Sawyer's knife that reads, "Family Is Forever." Nothing is more accurate than that. As a family, we've tried to balance my demanding job by making it fun with exciting, meaningful trips to IRONMAN races and walking the *Dolphin Tale* red carpets together. I'm eternally grateful for the extended family God has given me as well, all the way from my dad to both moms; my brothers, Rob, Randy, Dan, Mike and Elton; my sister, Katie, and our daughter-in-law, Andrea. Last but certainly not least, our ridiculously cute grandsons and future CEOs, Finley Jett Yates and Murphy Maverick Yates.

Grandson Fin Yates meeting Hope (Winter was nearby) – Dec 2019
(Come on, with a name like Fin, he had to meet them!)

The Village It Took!

Of all the amazing things that happened to me at CMA, it's the relationships I developed that take the prize. I had an excellent, inspirational staff and volunteers at CMA who continue to dazzle with their dedication and talent. I also gained many friends through filming both movies, including the cast and crew and the Alcon team.

The Alcon team has become more friends than partners since we were in the trenches together for two major motion pictures. Among my friends at Alcon are co-CEOs Andrew Kosove and Broderick Johnson. They and their families were wonderful and incredibly kind to me. Andrew and Broderick—both nominated for Oscars for *The Blind Side*—have incredibly generous hearts. The strong human message of the *Dolphin Tale* movies (that led to countless lives changed for the better) would never have happened without them. For them, it wasn't all about the money.

Then there is Scott Parish, the longtime Alcon CFO and the former Alcon staff of Dave Fierson, Steve Wegner, and Richard Ingber, among many others. They have all been fantastic to work with. Richard and his wife, Pam, remain close friends.

Line producer Bob Engelman was the one I worked with more than anyone else. He and his wife, Sarah, remain good friends to this day. In fact, one of their children, Alexis, is on the autism spectrum and is an inspiration to all who know her.

Bob Munroe (*The Expanse, The Tudors*), Noam Dromi (*The Walking Dead: Red Machete*), Ricou Browning (*The Glades, Graceland*) and Harvey Rosenstock (*Ray Donovan, Homeland*) have been a joy to work with and get to know. Jane Hassinger (*Graceland, Letters to God*), Jim Bigham (*Black Widow, Spider Man Far From Home*) and Bob Talbot (*Free Willy*) have become good friends. And, of course, working with director and long-term actor Charles Martin Smith (*American Graffiti, The Untouchables*) was a great honor.

My Friends: The Actors

But of all the great people I got to know through the movies, three have become very special friends. They are indeed family. Cozi Zuehlsdorff (Hazel), Nathan Gamble (Sawyer) and Austin Highsmith (Phoebe) and their families have all become a big part of CMA and my life. We first connected on the set of *Dolphin Tale,* and we each had our own providential journey that carried us to the movie set.

We became friends during filming, but the friendship didn't end after the wrap party. We kept in touch, and by the time we filmed *Dolphin Tale 2,* our friendships were cemented. The closeness we share didn't happen solely because we spent time together, but also because we share a similar faith and got to see the miracle of Winter's transformative influence on sick and injured kids. As I mentioned, the movie motto is "Family is Forever." And they are family too. The four of us have text chains going, keeping everyone up to date on what's happening in our lives. We keep in touch nearly daily and pray for each other and our families. I am genuinely one grateful man. Their parents, Scott & Allison Zuehlsdorff, Greg & Christy Gamble and Johnny & Dawn Highsmith, are great friends and amazing people. It's no wonder their kids are so successful.

Cozi, Nathan, Austin and me surprising four special needs kids with a job offer after graduation. All four have significant medical challenges.

Austin, me, Joan, Nathan and Cozi. I've been ridiculously blessed.

An Ending

On November 11, 2021, Winter the dolphin passed away after developing a severe intestinal issue. It is no coincidence that she passed away on Veterans Day, as she was her own warrior and inspired many wounded soldiers during her days at CMA. She packed more inspiration into her 16 years than most people could do in a hundred lifetimes. I am ever grateful that God gave her as a gift to the world and that He entrusted me with her story. The memories I have of the thousands of sick kids and wounded soldiers we worked with will never leave me. Swim on, sweet girl, you're swimming *downstream* now.

My Encouragement to You

Don't compare yourself to me or anyone else. Instead, lead your own BIG LIFE wherever you are and whatever you do. Become a better teacher, work harder at being a banker who looks out for the little guy, be a better neighbor, serve your community, put your skills to work in a ministry or nonprofit or find someone you can mentor. These are all ways to live BIG LIVES. Find the BIG LIFE that is yours and yours alone. Don't wait. I led the IRONMAN, brought Winter's story to the world, fought off an attack from Scientology (Google it), and fought corruption in the state of Georgia (a future book). YOU CAN ALSO DO BIG THINGS! Just take the first step.

Life is a precious gift. For reasons we won't understand this side of heaven, many people experience it through obstacles they didn't create, such as the many kids who have come to CMA searching for hope. Their lives have been filled with pain, surgeries, uncertainties and sorrow. They may never know what it's like to ride a bike or have a girlfriend or boyfriend, yet they fight to become beacons of hope for others. They are the true inspirations.

Chances are, you don't know me personally. But after reading this book, you know me at least a little bit. I want to take our last moment together to implore you to chase your dreams down with everything you have and turn them into reality. You were born for more. People need what God gave you.

As I finish writing this book, I do so with a smile, not for what I've been able to accomplish with the help of so many talented and compassionate people, but because one day I may meet you and you'll tell me about the BIG LIFE you went after because of what you read here. We'll talk, and once we're done, I'll turn around and smile much wider.

Dream and dream BIG. Live a BIG LIFE.

"For I know the plans I have for you," declares the LORD, "plans to prosper you and not to harm you, plans to give you hope and a future."

~Jeremiah 29:11

David & Winter, 2020

David Yates is available for speaking engagements, small business and nonprofitco nsulting and personal coaching. Learn more about David's inspirational work and other books and products at

DavidYatesInspire.com.

If you enjoyed the book, please drop a review on my Amazon book page. If you didn't like it, please don't. 🙂

APPENDIX

See these stories and more in David's upcoming book, *My Life with Winter the Dolphin*. Journeys of young overcomers from cystic fibrosis to cerebral palsy and autism to multiple organ transplants. Dive deep into the life-changing and life-saving inspiration of Winter the Dolphin and her fellow rescued friends at Clearwater Marine Aquarium.

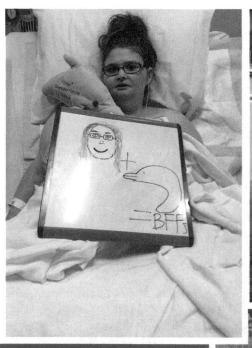

Special Appendix - Whale Rescue

When you are the CEO of a 24/7 marine life rescue center, you're kept on your toes in ways that are oftentimes stressful but also ridiculously rewarding. On July 29, 2019, about six months before I submitted my resignation to chase other dreams, our team got a call that five pilot (short-finned) whales had stranded themselves just a few miles down the road at a beautiful beach area named Redington Beach. This is one of Pinellas County's incredible white sand beaches, similar to Clearwater Beach. This rescue was in our rescue zone, so off we went. We also knew that these are public beaches, and it was peak tourism season, meaning this would not be hidden from the public. Our team arrived on the scene to hundreds gathered on the beach watching this spectacle of nature.

Why had these whales stranded themselves, how many were there, were there more coming? Our incredible team quickly organized the area, and due to the number and size of these animals, we decided to give the beachgoers a treat and let them assist with the rescue. Typically, we don't do this as caring for these animals takes significant experience, but in this case, we needed help and we got it.

Short-finned pilot whales are deep-water marine animals who mostly feed on squid at depths of 1,000 feet or more and are not commonly found close to shore. It was not immediately clear what caused the small group of pilot whales to beach themselves, but due to their social nature, it is possible that if even one animal is ill, the other companions may follow it to shore. Pilot whales are a species of cetaceans related to dolphins, which live in stable groups of 15 to 30 animals but can gather in social groups of hundreds. They may be dispersed over an area a half-mile wide while swimming together in search of food.

Short-finned pilot whales can weigh as much as three tons (males), but these five were varying sizes and weights. Working with our government partners, we made the decision that three of the five should be taken out for an immediate release, with the other two brought to our newly opened marine mammal rehabilitation facility in Tarpon Springs, Florida, just north of Clearwater. These two were both males, and the larger one was twelve feet long and weighed 1,603 pounds, while the "smaller" one was a mere ten feet and weighed just under 1,000 pounds.

There was extensive local and national media coverage for this unique event. The Tampa Bay community was enchanted by this inspiring story, and it led the news for more than a week. People couldn't get enough of these amazing animals and the attempt to rescue them. After three days of rehabilitation, in a late-night call, I had to give final sign-off on the release of the remaining two whales. I did so around 1 a.m. This put the release into motion, and around 9 a.m., we gathered north of Clearwater for the carefully planned release. We had to get the whales as far out as we could into the Gulf of Mexico to maximize their odds of success. We got them approximately 20 miles out and had the release. I was on the boat with them and it was an exhilarating experience, something most never get to be part of.

All five whales had been satellite tagged to monitor their movement and progress. We needed them to head to the deeper waters of the Gulf or they would be at risk all over again. For the next few weeks, we received daily tracking information on the whales.

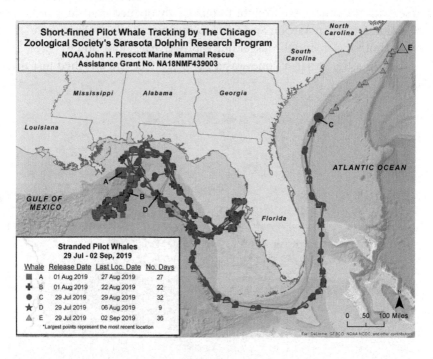

In the end, we do not know how each whale fared as the tracking eventually ended, but we are hopeful they all did well. The effort the CMA team and our partners and volunteers put forward was inspiring and hopeful. The community was touched, and during a time when the country seemed split, these whales amazingly brought us together. Below is the text of an editorial by the *Tampa Bay Times*:

> *Maybe those five pilot whales rescued us. It started, as so many emergencies do, with a 911 call. A worried beachgoer reported seeing whales splashing in the shallows of the Gulf of Mexico on Redington Beach and spouting through their blowholes. What happened next mattered more than the latest outrageous or outraged tweet or any cutting remark at one of the Democratic presidential debates last week: People came together, they took action, and they fixed a problem. We could use more of that.*
>
> *Those five whales needed help immediately. A small army of volunteers swung into action alongside marine biologists and veterinarians. The Clearwater Marine Aquarium, the National Oceanic and Atmospheric Administration, Coast Guard officers and the Florida Fish and Wildlife Conservation Commission were all involved.*
>
> *People set up shades to protect the whales as the searing sun rose high into the sky. Once experts determined the whales were healthy enough to move, the humans teamed up, hefting each one in a canvas sling, more than a dozen people per whale. The three larger whales were taken to deeper, safer waters by boat. The effort lasted 10 hours. The two younger males, simply called A and B, were driven to a Clearwater Marine Aquarium facility in Tarpon Springs for treatment.*
>
> *By late last week, A and B were well enough to be released, taken 20 miles out into the Gulf of Mexico. And by that time, the three older whales had already swum nearly 70 miles southwest. Radio tags will monitor their movements for several weeks.*
>
> *Whale beachings are rare, and usually don't end well. This one apparently has, and there are lessons.*
>
> *"Collaboration really works," Clearwater Marine Aquarium CEO David Yates told reporters at a news conference. "The community really got involved in this. One group can't do this the right way by themselves."*
>
> *He is right. In a time when people too readily deny science, experts and scientists helped save the day. In an era when people too often distrust each other, volunteers didn't separate into red teams or blue teams. They came together because, as a proverb common across many cultures says, many hands make light work.*

"It was really hard work," Thomas Nuhfer, a 27-year-old student from Clearwater who helped carry one of the whales, told the Times. "But it was so great to see people who didn't even know each other come together and work together to help."

Those five whales beached themselves on the shores of Pinellas County. On Nov. 8, 2016, half of Pinellas voters made a different choice than you did. President Donald Trump received 5,500 more votes than Hillary Clinton, but neither candidate broke 50 percent among the nearly half-million people who voted. With the polarization of politics in this country, it's too easy for citizens to walk down the sidewalk and count every second person they pass as an enemy rather than a fellow American. Had that happened on Redington Beach, those whales wouldn't be doing swimmingly.

They would be dead.

PHOTO CREDITS

Clearwater Marine Aquarium: 16, 65, 66, 67, 68, 70, 71, 75, 77, 80, 81, 82, 83, 84, 93, 95, 99, 101, 102, 103, 103, 104, 104, 105, 113, 116, 117, 119, 122, 139, 139, 145, 152, 153, 156, 158, 162, 174

Rich Cruse: 34, 36, 38, 40, 44

Carol Hogan/IRONMAN: 35

Terry Jordan: 49

Alem International: 55

Warner Bros.: 79, 94, 98, 109, 121

Pete Inman: 86

Toni Gross: 151

Tampa Bay Times: 88

Kimberly Larochelle: 108, 110

Bob Talbot: 115, book cover

Jena W. Frodsham: 140, 141

Natalie Guignard: 124, 127

Paul Marek: 144

Daniel Neu: 147

Cheryl Sitton: 149

CBMC: 165

Picture montage: Various parents

NOAA John H. Prescott Marine Mammal Rescue Assistance Grant No. NA18NMF439003: 172

Citations:
1. *Schizophrenia*: Oxford Languages
2. *Devastation*: Merriam–Webster
3. *Blue-sky*: Oxford Languages[175]
4. *Passion*: Oxford Languages

Made in the USA
Columbia, SC
26 June 2022